Everlasting Voices

Everlasting Voices:

Aspects of the Modern Irish Short Story

by
Richard J. Thompson

The Whitston Publishing Company
Troy, New York
1989

Permission from *Éire-Ireland* to reprint Chapters 2 and 4, which appeared there in slightly different form, is gratefully acknowledged, as is the receipt of research grants from Canisius College in 1979 and 1986.

For my families

Contents

Preface

In the five chapters that follow, I outline the major contributions made to the form of the twentieth-century Irish short story by George Moore and James Joyce and then examine the products of those I consider to be its four main practitioners. My attempt is to characterize the work of Frank O'Connor, Sean O'Faolain, Liam O'Flaherty, and Mary Lavin by theme and style and to trace the artistic development of each. Thus this is not a history of the Irish short story nor a story-by-story examination of each writer's output but rather a selective analysis and comparison of the best and most typical work that has appeared in the form.

Richard J. Thompson

Chapter One

In the First Place: *The Untilled Field* and *Dubliners*

1. The modern Irish short story begins with two books published early in this century, one almost unknown and the other perhaps unmatched in the genre in fame: George Moore's *The Untilled Field* (1903) and James Joyce's *Dubliners* (1914).[1] Moore's volume is neglected except for an occasional anthologist's dip into it as an act of nostalgic courtesy. Yet this pioneer work, as Vivian Mercier and others have noted,[2] allows us to see the crystallization of the Irish story teller's, or *shanachie's*, art in written form. Moore, though a child of the gentry, stayed close in this collection of thirteen stories to the plain roots of Mayo, to cottage and peasant and country priest. It is one of the ironies of Irish writers that on the other hand, Joyce, whose family social position was less exalted, imposed on the Irish short story form aspirations to much richer literary elegance.

The Irish have long enjoyed a deserved reputation for cameo work—the Tara brooch, the Ardagh chalice, the memorable tune, the exquisite oratory, and, in literature, the lyric poem, the one-act play, and the short story. They are, as Liam Miller has said, "a nation of miniaturists in perfection in the arts."[3] The *shanachie* was also a miniaturist. Nightly, over the long winter months, he proffered stories from his copious store, each story an embroidered anecdote, an expanded tidbit. Moore's originality in *The Untilled Field* lies in his developing the anecdote into a plain but complete narrative. Joyce, on the other hand, by integrating the techniques of French and Russian short story practitioners, epitomized the gains made in nineteenth-century continental tradition and technique.

In the beginning for the Irish fiction writer was the anecdote. As Thomas Kilroy puts it:

> At the centre of Irish fiction is the anecdote. The distinctive feature of our first novel, *Castle Rackrent*, that which makes it what it is, is not so much its idea, revolutionary as that may be, as its imitation of a speaking voice engaged in the telling of a tale. The model will be exem-

> plary for the reader who has read widely in Irish fiction; it
> is a voice heard over and over again, whatever its accent, *a*
> *voice* with a supreme confidence in its own histrionics, *one*
> *that assumes with its audience a shared ownership of the told tale*
> *and all that this implies:* a taste for anecdote, an unshakeable
> belief in the value of human actions, a belief that life may
> be adequately encapsulated into stories that require no
> reference, no qualification, beyond their own selves.[4]

Anecdotalism is the first cousin of gossip, in which tone is used in such a way as to convey character information about both the narrating speaker and his subject. Concomitantly, Frank O'Connor, the principal Irish theoretician of the short story, stipulates in a well-known phrase that the short story must ring with "the tone of a man's voice, speaking."[5] Both Kilroy's and O'Connor's aspects of anecdotalism emphasize the speaking voice of the teller. These two aspects are reflected in the characteristic oral nature of the majority of the stories in *The Untilled Field*.

The *Untilled Field* and *Dubliners* reflect, respectively, oral and written tradition, local and European influence, rural and urban culture. The polarized strains exemplified by these two collections did not come together in Irish story writing practice for several decades, not with consistency, in fact, until the internationalist type of story— that written by the later O'Faolain, Mary Lavin, Aidan Higgins, and Edna O'Brien—began to appear after World War II.

In 1900, Moore's resentment of British colonialism was so intensified by British ruthlessness in the Boer War that he left London. He was attracted back to Ireland by the efforts of Douglas Hyde's Gaelic League to restore the Irish language as an important tongue. Although, like Yeats and Joyce, he knew almost no Irish, he had heard it spoken throughout his youth in Mayo and was sentimentally devoted to its restoration. "I came to give Ireland back her language," he told AE with typical flair and *hauteur*. He wrote his stories at the beginning of the flood tide of the literary revival and at the urging of the cultural nationalist, John Eglinton, knowing they would be published first in Irish and hoping they might be used as school texts for the teaching of that language. (It was a surprising hope when one considers the then-shocking material in the opening story—young Lucy Delaney posing in the nude for a statute of the Blessed Virgin Mary.) After three of the stories were published separately in the nationalistic *New Ireland Review*, the collected volume was published in Irish in 1902 under the title *An T-ur-Gort, Sgealta*.

The author's countrymen paid minimal attention to the edition in English in 1903—the book sold hardly a hundred copies in its first year. Moore was practically alone in calling it, as its title hinted, "a landmark in Anglo-Irish literature, a new departure."[6] And yet, in total effect, the work is as subversive in treating *fin-de-siecle* Irish life as Joyce's. Over and over, Moore's stories reflect the meanness and bleakness of country life: life dominated by the parish priest, the disappearance of a superior past, the necessity of exile. "In every one," Moore wrote his publisher, "there is a priest and Ireland is represented as a sort of modern Tibet."[7] Brendan Kennelly correctly detects the overall burden of *The Untilled Field* to be "a scrutiny of spiritual inertia just as *Dubliners* is an exposition of various kinds of paralysis."[8]

Thus, here is the way the young artist, John Rodney, judges his native land at the end of the original version of the opening story, "In the Clay":

> 'Oh, the ignorance, the crass, the patent ignorance! I am going. This is no place for a sculptor to live in. It is no country for an educated man. It won't be fit for a man to live in for another hundred years. It is an unwashed country, that is what it is!'[9]

Or consider "The Wild Goose," the longest story in the volume, which contains what Malcolm Brown has called "Moore's own definitive statement on the Irish soul."[10] Ned, about to leave Ireland, takes down in musical notation a shepherd's tune played on the flageolet, and finds in it "the song of exile; it is the cry of one driven out into the night . . . and the exile is on the edge of waste. . . . It is a prophetic echo and final despair of a people who knew they were done for from the beginning" (p. 355). Here Moore synthesizes what would become the dual theme running through the modern Irish short story: lament and protest. In fact, Moore thought that his perpetual themes of disaffection and exile later influenced Synge's endings to *The Playboy of the Western World* and *Riders to the Sea*. For Moore's stories express the heart-scalding frustration in Irish life that always threatens to become self-hate. It would be hard to improve on David Marcus' list of "Irish malaises," and *The Untilled Field* utilizes almost all of them:

> . . . the massive burden of a baleful history, the catastrophic disaster of famines that reduced the population by half, the sickening and unquenchable draining off of the youth to America and Britain, the demeaning shame of the death of

> a native language and the silting up of ancient traditions,
> the oedipal rendings of Irish manhood's father-hatred and
> mother-fixation, and the formative repressions of a strict
> religious and moral code operating within the narrow
> boundaries of a predominately rural society that influ-
> enced every second of one's waking life. So when an Irish
> short story protests, it is more often than not the keening of
> a nation.[11]

Although the subject matter of Moore's volume is vindictive
and seditious, his technique continues the conventional story teller's
spoken art. As we've said, the tenor of the stories bespeak their origin
in *anecdota*, in "things unpublished," in oral roots on which the Irish
printed story drew more than any other branch of European literature
except the Yiddish. The three characteristic marks of the anecdote—
a preference for entertainment over artistic arrangement, a penchant
for the preternatural, for levitating a little, and an emphasis on the
personal or "gossipy"—are completely in evidence here. In Frank
O'Connor's opinion, an ideal short story might begin: "By the hokies,
there was a man in this place one time by the name of Ned Sullivan,
and a queer thing happened him late one night and he coming up the
Valley Road from Durlas."[12] But a Moore opening can be just as chatty
and magnetic: "'It's a closed mouth that can hold a good story,' as the
saying goes, and very soon it got about that Father Mac Turnan had
written to Rome saying that he was willing to take a wife to his bosom
for patriotic reasons, if the Pope would relieve him of the vow of
celibacy" ("A Play-House in the Waste"). Or: "One morning the priest's
housekeeper mentioned as she gathered up the breakfast things, that
Mike Mulhare had refused to let his daughter Catherine marry James
Murdoch until he had earned the price of a pig" ("A Letter to Rome").

Kilroy observes that, if anecdote is the center of Irish fiction,
fantasy is its periphery.[13] Moore was steeped in fantasy and in legends
of the supernatural. In the words of one commentator:

> Celtic mysticism was familiar to him from childhood; he
> had been brought up on Mayo legends, and Moore Hall
> had its own history of supernatural events ... Indeed, what
> passes as psychological interest in Moore's later works is
> often remarkably close to the personality changes, inner
> and outer compulsions, and related themes that abound in
> Irish folklore.[14]

Thus it is not surprising to see in a number of stories how far Moore, in middle age, had retreated from the influence of Zola and French realism: in "The Wedding Gown," a young girl telepathically detects her grandmother's hour of death. In "The Clerk's Quest," the protagonist, as he dies, knows himself to be "passing into a diviner sense" (p. 245). In "So On He Fares," the youthful son is magically cloned after his older self runs off to sea.

Moore's anecdotal art combines sharp social criticism with fluent expression—in sum, he rejects Boucicault's Amos-and-Andy dialect and the forelock-tugging just then emerging in Lady Gregory's Kiltartan stories. In *The Untilled Field*, as elsewhere, Moore's style is plain—he is one of English literature's natural writers, an urbane man who wrote plainly. "He carries us on when we read him," A. Norman Jeffares states, "and that is perhaps the secret of the enjoyment he can give: it is the art of the story teller he develops and he appeals to our common delight in, and enjoyment of, a story well told."[15] The conversational voice and use of local settings and customs do not coincide with the print-oriented century ahead but cling instead to the orality of tone that predated it.

Moore did not further cultivate the field to which he had opened the way. In his later collections of short stories, *A Storyteller's Holiday* (1918) and *Celibate Lives* (1927), he returned to the manner of the continental art story, the *conte*, and to the polished literary style that clothes his novels and memoirs. But *The Untilled Field* deserves to loom large in any retrospective evaluation of Moore's work, for it provided a model for his successors to explore the life of *rural* Ireland at a time when it was becoming unfashionable to admit the "truth [that] ours is still a rural country," as the poet Hugh Maxton stated in his "Ode" of the 1970's. In each decade since *The Untilled Field* appeared, there has been a harvest of the anecdotal-oral-rural story, starting with Seamus O'Kelly and Daniel Corkery and carrying on through Liam O'Flaherty, Michael McLaverty, and Bryan MacMahon, among many others.

2. The modern Irish art-story of subtle psychological effect and symbol, couched in esoteric vocabulary ("gnomon," "spondulics," "minsters" of jelly), sprang from Joyce's mandarin brow. No Irish book remotely like *Dubliners* existed before it, no work blending such an array of what had been thought of as continental qualities: the *sec*

sprightliness of Daudet, Chekov's compassion, Gogol's narrative drive and eye for the grotesque in the everyday, Flaubert's precision of style, a style offering to the ear English sentences modulated with the sensitivity of a trained singer. H. E. Bates aptly labelled *Dubliners* a "solitary, delicate, and long-unwanted volume."[16] While each adjective is meet, the first is most cogent, for Joyce turned away from the spirit of his age and place, from the folkishness of Hyde's *Love Songs of Connaught* and Yeats' *Celtic Twilight,* from the central English short story tradition of Kipling, Wells, and Bennett. In their place, he chose Flaubertian elegance.

It is often said that *Dubliners* reflects Joyce's feelings of hurt and anger toward his paralyzed country. We have been led to imagine him chortling when his seditious stories were published by the unsuspecting AE between the fertilizer ads in the *Irish Statesman.* But it is much more important to see that they are urban equivalents of Gray's "Elegy," respectful records of lives lived with courage and forbearance amid many kinds of hardship and squalor. The theme of *Dubliners* is not so much political castigation as the pitifulness of life: the main emphasis is on the need for courage on the part of Little Chandler or Maria, on the terrible helplessness of Eveline, Bob Doran, Farrington, and Mr. James Duffy. Theirs are the short and simple annals of the poor, especially the poor in spirit; politics will come later with Stephen Dedalus and his nefarious nets. Stephen, however, in the *Portrait* is something of a prig, not at one with the lost souls of *Dubliners* who look forward more properly to the tragically joyous Bloom.

Joyce's literary devices in *Dubliners* are invariably drawn from the high culture of western literary tradition—irony, satire, parody (including mock epic), rhetorical figures such as paradox, periphrasis, puns, and alliteration. He is not random—no breath is ever wasted. Protagonist's questions lead in due time to epiphanies ("Could he write something original?"; "Why had he withheld life from her? Why had he sentenced her to death?"; '*What am I to do?*:' "Did he pay you yet?"; "Did you try her?"; "Isn't it a terrible thing to die so young as that?"). The wily question-asker contrasts to the homely surrogate *shanachie* of *The Untilled Field.* Moore's flowing plainness has no counterpart in Joyce where a single action may be a microcosm of a larger totality such as a person's life or the eternal life-process, where river, park, and city function as time, innocence, and experience, and where a motif, an allusion, or image may evoke whole layers of suggestion.

One supposedly simple motif from *Dubliners* might be chosen to illustrate Joyce's interweaving artfulness and high craft, namely his use of the metaphor of gaming or playing, in its multiplicity of connotations, which is plaited through the book to organize character and signal character change, usually from innocence to the pain of mature insight.[17] Thus Maloney, according to the old josser in "An Encounter," "is different; he goes in for games" (p. 25).[18] Indeed, he goes in for chasing and stoning cats and "brandishing his . . . catapult," (p. 22) the last of which is sexual slang for the old josser's own perverted game. But the game image is crucial to the point of the story: the bookish narrator *is* different from the screaming yahoo Maloney and lucklessly like the repulsive oldster. Play is also used to presage an unpleasant realization in "Araby." There the narrator leaves behind the "career of [his] play" (p. 30) to confront the sobering bazaar of life and its seedy Café Chantant where the money-grubbers lurk. His bibulous and insincere uncle's bromide about "All work and no play" (p. 34) is a preparation for the general insincerity of the adult world. The lonely drudgery of Eveline's life in the story of that name—she forsakes marriage and children to wait on her whining widower father—is hinted at again through the image of play by Joyce when he tells us that Eveline used "to play every evening with other people's children" (p. 36). So will it be for her in perpetuity.

But Joyce goes on to use play or gaming to effect even larger suggestions than the encroaching tribulations of growing up. In "After the Race," during the card game on the Belle of Newport, Jimmy Doyle, standing for Ireland, is retired to the role of witless onlooker whose patrimony is usurped by the representatives of England and France ("Jimmy understood that the game lay between Routh and Segouin," p. 48). The card game becomes a re-enactment of Irish national history with Jimmy playing the part of the ultimate grand loser. From playing cards Joyce goes to playing music in "Two Gallants"—the weary harpist's one hand "played in the base the melody of *Silent, O Moyle,* while the other hand careered in the treble after each set of notes" (p. 54). The begging street artist's hand strokes but cannot excite: the image depicts the national state of the arts. This parodic gesture is caricatured by Lenehan when later he absently strokes the silent railings around the Duke's Lawn. Presumably, Corley is fondling the slavey at the same time. All loves are sordid in this story, all gold fool's gold, all music mute or dissonant. Going with decent girls, as Lenehan says, is "a mug's game" (p. 52).

Bob Doran is himself the game or quarry ("He had a notion he was being had," p. 66) in "The Boarding House," though the "Madam" compounds the image when she counts all her "cards" before sending for him, feeling sure "she would win" (p. 65). In this story and others, playing becomes a metaphor for manipulating people into doing what one wants. Jack Mooney stands menacingly by to see that Polly gets her cracker, ensuring that no one will try "that sort of game on with *his* sister" (p. 68). In "A Little Cloud," Ignatius Gallaher is as calculating as the "Madam," being resolved to avoid Little Chandler's failure in marriage by marrying someone wealthy ("See if I don't play my cards properly" p. 81), while Farrington in "Counterparts" loses his reputation as a strong man and his ideal of himself as a playboy when he loses the hand-wrestling game to the knockabout artiste, Weathers. His lost ability to drink, to hand-wrestle, to play in general, underscores the tackiness of his life.

In another contest, Maria picks the clod of clay and both wins and loses the blindman's-bluff game in "Clay." Since she is a veritable peacemaker, she suffers without complaint when made to stand beside the piano and sing. The forced and scorned performance dramatizes her mocked solitude. Playing as social charade, as music raucous or too faint, as cheap trick, is a continuous element and linking device throughout *Dubliners*.

Consider, very quickly, two more instances of musical playing. Although Mr. James Duffy briefly leaves off playing his solitary piano in "A Painful Case," he soon returns to it, an outcast from life's feast. He prefers watching someone else play, in the concert hall or in the shadow of the wall of Phoenix Park, to crossing the line and making a play for Emily Sinico. Duffy prefers artifice and solitary play to participation and contact with others. Hardly less aloof and austere, though a great deal more forceful, is Mrs. Kearney in "A Mother" whose "playing and ivory manners were much admired" (136) in her youth, but who now plays at a sort of sleight-of-hand, keeping the audience continually diverted by slipping "the doubtful items in between the old favourites" (p. 138). The playing of music, of cards, of games, is equated with duplicity. "Did you ever see this little trick?" (p. 130) asks Mr. Henchy in "Ivy Day in The Committee Room" as he sets the "tardy" corks before the fireplace. His parlor-trick produces the three-*pok* salute that burlesques even as it reveals the general seediness of the political gamesters who have followed in Parnell's wake.

Finally, in the last two stories, Joyce offers exercises in grown-up play-acting as social rite. In "Grace," three men (they hope to make a "four-handed reel,"p. 163) visit Tom Kernan's sick-bed in order to gull him toward the supposedly salubrious influence of Father Purdom, the spiritual accountant. Martin Cunningham's play-acting credentials extend to his face, which resembles Shakespeare's. Kernan, nearly fork-tongued, only plays at drinking tea—he spits it out—as Harford only plays at being a Jew for business gain. Jack Power resents McCoy's "low playing of the game" (p. 166) when McCoy borrows baggage for his wife to use on her "imaginary" singing engagements in the country. From the game of cabbage-catching to the ferociously played contest of seeing who can best hyperbolize the Catholic hierarchy ("...at last the Pope himself stood up and declared infallibility a dogma of the Church *ex cathedra*...." p. 169), "Grace" is an hilarious exposure of pretentiousness and gamesmanship.

In "The Dead," the stage is full of corpses jerking to the accustomed strings of social politeness and feigning vitality. The Three Graces, two of them all but moribund, play at music; Lily *used* to play on the lowest step with her rag doll, but now she too is "not the girl she was at all" (p. 181). In referring to his aunts and cousin, Gabriel says that he "will not attempt to play tonight the role that Paris played" (p. 204): for all of them, the music is over, except for academy pieces. The whole *tableau* of the party is frozen, out of time. The pictures on the wall, portraying scenes from Shakespeare's plays, don't move, just as Gretta is transfixed into "Distant Music." "Who's playing up there?" asks Gabriel, and the answer comes, "Nobody. They're all gone" (p. 206). The playing is done; the vast hosts of the dead hover immaterially just out of reach, "done for" like the Irish whom George Moore describes dolefully in "The Wild Goose." But in contrast to Moore, the author of *Dubliners* is himself ghostly, refined out of existence, leaving only the telling itself, an impersonal voice spinning out the web of story in the museyroom of the imagination.

Dubliners, finally published by Grant Richards thirteen days before the shooting of Archduke Ferdinand, was greeted with solid admiration by readers and critics. Commentators regularly compared it to French and Russian antecedents; the only writer in English mentioned repeatedly as likely to have influenced the collection is—George Moore. There can be no doubt that the major influences on Joyce were foreign,[19] chiefly Chekhov (whom Joyce most likely read in 1903, the year before Chekhov's death) and, more important still,

Flaubert, whose focus in *Madam Bovary*, "La Legende de St. Julien le Hospitalier," and *La Tentation de Saint Antoine* is so often, like Joyce's in *Dubliners*, upon the meanness and disillusionment of *bourgeois* life.

Both Moore and Joyce no doubt were jointly attentive to Arthur Symon's *The Symbolist Movement in Literature* (1899), a book of considerable importance to the English-speaking literary world of its day, as critics from T. S. Eliot to Cyril Connolly have asserted.[20] In truth, Moore's three portrait-stories in *Celibates* (1895) reflect a precision and luminosity that look forward to the tenets of his friend Symon's work. *The Untilled Field* is another matter; nothing serves to elucidate the difference between it and *Dubliners* so sharply as a consideration of how the former ignores and the latter utilizes the symbolic techniques first adumbrated by Symons. Incidentally, in 1914 Joyce sent a copy of *Dubliners* to Symons and got an immediate favorable reply saying that the stories offered "a kind of French realism,"[21] to Symons' mind the highest praise.

The contributions of *Dubliners* to the world short story are universally admitted but variously particularized. No doubt *Dubliners* helped to write *finis* to the story of rural ambience, though the best later books of American stories, *In Our Time* and *Winesburg, Ohio*, continued to ignore the city. No doubt *Dubliners* is historically a prism through which the subject matter of Chekhov and the careful technique of Flaubert were made accessible in English and blended by Joyce with his own distinctive gifts for psychological penetration, satiric empathy, polymorphic language, and crossroads endings.

In extending the foregoing distinction between Moore and Joyce, between the story teller and the story writer, into the next generation, one should name Frank O'Connor as the most powerful propagator of the story teller's mode and Sean O'Faolain as the most accomplished stylist and writer. (Obviously such distinctions grow academic and tenuous as the oral story teller becomes extinct and prose technique, including that of the short story, becomes increasingly hermeneuticized.) Abundant traces of *Dubliners* and of Joyce in general are to be found in the first four of O'Faolain's eight volumes of short stories. Besides the works of O'Faolain, one can see the clear influence of *Dubliners* in John Montague's regrettably slighted collection *Death of a Chieftain* (1964), in Aidan Higgin's *Felo de Se* (1961), and in the stories of writers as different from each other as John McGahern and Samuel Beckett.

3. A word about the relationship, professional and personal, of Moore and Joyce. They sniped and sniffed at one another's work over the course of thirty-two years, starting with the 19-year-old Joyce's first upstart notice of Moore in "The Day of the Rabblement" in 1901 (" . . . however frankly Mr. Moore may quote Pater and Turgenieff to defend himself, his new impulse has no kind of relation to the future of art")[22] and continuing until Moore's death in 1933. Probably as a result of his youthful affront, Joyce was denied invitation to Moore's at-homes on Ely Place, a rebuke noted in the library episode of *Ulysses*. When in 1903 AE showed him some of Joyce's poems, Moore dismissed them with the contemptuous snort, "Symons,"[23] an accurate offhand correlation. The next ripostes were Joyce's. He called Moore "damned stupid" in a letter of 1904 to his brother Stanny for having a character in *The Untilled Field* look up the train schedule from Bray to Dublin, a needless act for a native, Joyce thought, since the trains ran on a regular schedule.[24] In another letter to Stanny, in 1906, Joyce skewered Moore's novel *The Lake* for being pretentious and unintentionally funny.[25] The hero, Father Oliver Gogarty, drops his priestly clothes on one side of the lake and, swimming to the other, begins an altogether new life. One wonders if Joyce wasn't "correcting" Moore's favorable portrait of Gogarty in *The Lake* when he pictured the plunging "usurper," Buck Mulligan, in the Forty-Foot in *Ulysses*.

Joyce's 1904 letter to Stanny indicates that he had read, with qualified appreciation, *The Untilled Field*; there is likewise evidence that Moore had looked, with qualified appreciation, into *Dubliners*. Asked in 1916 by Prime Minister Asquith's secretary for his opinion of Joyce's work when Joyce was being considered for a Civil List pension, Moore replied:

> The only book of Joyce's that I have read is a collection of stories called 'Dubliners,' some of them are trivial and disagreeable, but all are written by a clever man, and the book contains one story, the longest story in the book and the last story which seemed to me perfection whilst I read it! I regretted that I was not the author of it. But this story, which I'm sure you would appreciate as much as I did, does not prove that Joyce will go on writing and will end by writing something like a masterpiece. A talent, musical, literary, or pictorial, is a pale fluttering thing that a breath will extinguish.[26]

The closing characterization of the artist-as-delicate-butterfly conflicts rudely with Joyce's then published portrait of the artist as a person of Daedalian determination and commitment, willing to live by silence, exile, and cunning. It is a strange image of Joyce for Moore to infer, but then Joyce's view of Moore, expressed a few years earlier in "Gas from a Burner," as "a genuine gent / That lives on his property's ten percent," is a no-less-superficial picture, this time of Moore's effeteness. Moore, who was thirty years older than Joyce and who grew more crapulous and dandified in his last decade of life, dismissed Joyce shortly after the appearance of *Ulysses* as "a sort of Zola gone to seed.... Joyce, why he's nobody—from the Dublin docks: no family, no breeding...his *Portrait of the Artist as a Young Man* [is] a book entirely without style or distinction; why, I did the same thing, but much better, in *The Confessions of a Young Man*."[27]

It is amusing and saddening to notice how Moore and Joyce reacted to one another with typical Irish class venom ("...lives on his property's ten percent"; "...from the Dublin docks"). Joseph Hone, in his biography of Moore, quotes a lengthy and fascinating unpublished memoir by Barrett Clark which includes details of an accidental meeting between the two writers in a Paris restaurant in 1922 when Moore was in his seventieth year. Once again, the social question of money intrudes: Moore has just dismissed Hardy's novels ("I recall that absurd scene in *Tess of the* -er- that *Tess* book....") and "invented a scandalous anecdote about Watts-Dunton, [when] James Joyce entered the restaurant, and sitting down, looked at Moore out of one eye, the other being covered with a black patch. Moore stared at him and then inquired in a stage whisper if 'that' was Joyce, and how he made his living."[28] Nothing ensued; they genially cut each other, Joyce on the eve of publishing *Ulysses* and just becoming a cult figure to other, especially younger, writers, and Moore having just published *his* rendition of past legend after the manner of Dujardin's, *Héloise and Abélard*. The Shem and Shaun of the Irish short story in Les Deux Magots.

When the two finally met formally in London in 1929, Joyce was polite to the point of obsequiousness, perhaps put off by Moore's *hauteur*. Moore noticed, as no doubt Joyce did also, the rough parallels of their lives and careers, and yet the congenital dissimilarities. Moore wrote of the meeting in a letter to Eglinton:

> He was distinguished, courteous, respectful, and I was the
> same. He seemed anxious to accord me first place. I
> demurred, and declared him first in Europe. We agreed

that our careers were not altogether dissimilar.... I said I
have been only a revolutionary, while you have been a
heroic revolutionary, for *you* had no money.[29]

They had come a long way from the stark fields of Mayo and the
circuitous streets of Dublin.

Notes

[1] *Dubliners*, except for "The Dead," was completed in 1906. Joyce's battles
with Grant Richards and the Mssrs. Maunsel to have his stories published as a
collection then began.

[2] See Mercier's Introduction to *Great Irish Short Stories* (New York: Dell
Publishing Company, 1964) 13.

[3] Liam Miller, "The Future of Irish Poetry," *The Irish Times*, February 5, 1970,
14.

[4] Thomas Kilroy, "Irish Writing Today," *Times Literary Supplement*, 17 March
1972. Italics Kilroy's.

[5] Frank O'Connor, Foreword to *Stories by Frank O'Connor* (New York:
Vintage Books, 1956), vii.

[6] George Moore, Preface to *The Untilled Field* (Toronto: The MacMillan
Company of Canada Limited, 1976), xxi-xxii. This Preface was not included in the
early editions of the book.

[7] Moore, quoted in *George Moore in Transition, Letters to T. Unwin Fisher and
Lena Milman, 1894-1910*, ed. by Helmut E. Gerber (Detroit: Wayne State University
Press, 1968) 247. Gerber correctly points out that there is no priest in the eighth story,
"The Wedding Gown."

[8] Brendan Kennelly, in *George Moore's Mind and Art*, ed. by Graham Owens
(Edinburgh: Oliver and Boyd, 1968) 153.

[9] Moore, *The Untilled Field* (Philadelphia: J. B. Lippincott, 1903), 29. Page
numbers after quotations refer to this text. This is the first American edition.

[10] Malcolm Brown, *George Moore, a Reconsideration* (Seattle: University of
Washington Press, 1955) 173.

[11] David Marcus, Introduction to *Modern Irish Short Stories* (London: Sphere
Books Limited, 1972) 12-13.

[12] Frank O'Connor, *The Lonely Voice* (Cleveland and New York: The World
Publishing Company, 1962) 13.

[13] Kilroy, *loc cit.*

[14] Janet Egleson Dunleavy, *George Moore: The Artist's Vision, The Storyteller's
Art* (Lewisburg, PA: Bucknell University Press, 1973) 118-119.

[15] A. Norman Jeffares, *George Moore*, in the *Writers and Their Works* Series, No. 180 (London: Longman, Green and Company, 1965) 38.

[16] H. E. Bates, *The Modern Short Story: A Critical Survey* (London: Thomas Nelson and Sons, 1945) 15.

[17] Christopher Lauer speaks of Joyce's "ludic" propensities in *Ulysses* and *Finnegans Wake* in the *James Joyce Quarterly*, 12:4 (Summer, 1975) 423-435.

[18] Page numbers after quotations refer to *Dubliners* (New York: The Viking Press, 1961).

[19] Marvin Magalaner and Richard Kain have enumerate a number of the influences on *Dubliners* in "*Dubliners* and the Short Story," in *James Joyce's Dubliners, A Critical Handbook*, ed. by James Baker and Thomas Staley (Belmont, CA: Wadsworth Publishing Company, 1969) 16-28.

[20] See, *e.g.*, Cyril Connolly's testimonial to Symon's book in *The Evening Colonnade* (New York: Harcourt, Brace, Jovanovish, 1975), 155 *et seq.*

[21] Arthur Symons, quoted in *James Joyce: The Critical Heritage, I*, ed. by Robert Deming (New York: Barnes and Noble, 1970), 59.

[22] James Joyce, *The Critical Writings of James Joyce*, ed. by Ellsworth Mason and Richard Ellmann (New York: The Viking Press, 1959) 71.

[23] Quoted by Richard Ellmann in *James Joyce*, (Oxford University Press, 1965), 140.

[24] James Joyce, *Letters of James Joyce*, Volume II, ed. by Richard Ellmann (New York: The Viking Press, 1966) 71.

[25] Joyce, *Letters*, II, 154.

[26] Quoted in Ellmann's *James Joyce*, p. 418. Moore concluded the letter with a postscript saying that, "from a literary point of view Joyce is deserving of help" (419), and so, with Yeats' support and Pound's connivance, the Prime Minister granted Joyce £100.

[27] Ellmann, *James Joyce* 543-44.

[28] Joseph Hone, *The Life of George Moore*, (New York: The Macmillan Company, 1936) 376.

[29] Quoted in Ellmann, *James Joyce* 630.

Chapter Two

A Kingdom of Commoners: The Moral Art of Frank O'Connor

Frank O'Connors' first four volumes are the real achievements in the Irish short story after the form crystalized a generation before in *The Untilled Field* and *Dubliners*. O'Connor deserves to be recognized not only as an artist who synthesized the ruralism and anecdotalism of Moore with the urbanity and psychological penetration of Joyce, but also as the mediator of the provincialism of the *shanachie* and the internationalism running from O'Faolain to Higgins. The purpose here is to examine the special flavor and manner of those four volumes —thereafter O'Connor's work declines in merit and distinction—in order to weigh his artistic importance. The volumes in question are *Guests of the Nation* (1931), *Bones of Contention* (1936), *Crab Apple Jelly* (1944), and *The Common Cord* (1947).

O'Connor was a dogged craftsman, a perfectionist, an indefatigable rewriter and self-second-guesser—all habits he shared with James Joyce, as he did a devotion to deep learning of diverse sorts. Yet O'Connor branded Joyce as "the first of the Ph.D. novelists." *Dubliners* was to him an example of how not to write short stories, for it preferred characterization over a quality that O'Connor thought prime: incident, which he called theme. Accordingly, a character named Joyce in O'Connor's story "What's Wrong with the Country?" is described as "a small, stocky obstinate fellow with a precise and cynical mind." The polite encomia for *Dubliners* in *The Lonely Voice* aside, O'Connor found Joyce's short story technique more trivial than quadrivial.

In contradistinction, O'Connor's work is characterized by a yearning to recapture something lost—primal order or an older decency that has been overriden by social duty or, perhaps, a childhood of ineffable simplicity and trust. Ultimately, like Sean O'Casey, O'Connor is an Oedipist who discerns a better world before the advent of striving and grief. His longing for order, decency, and love suggests his intense moralism which, along with a tone of unshakable equanimity, gives his stories their principal trademark. O'Connor says in *An Only Child* that, while he did not believe in the immortality of his own soul, he did believe in that of some souls, doubtless his mother's, and so "perhaps it was the thought of these [souls] that turned me finally from poetry to story-telling, to the celebration of those who for me represented all I should ever know of god."[1]   But these very characteristics engender his worst faults—a lack of complexity, occasionally muddy and ill-conceived plots, and a cloying nostalgic cheerfulness, what Walter Allen has called O'Connor's persistent stance of "What an interesting little boy I once was!" Temperamentally, O'Connor's vision was directed backwards to the time, recounted in his autobiography, when he was Michael O'Donovan from Blarney Lane. "Look back to look forward," he writes in his dedication to *The Backward Look*. And since his tendency is Oedipal, the habitual frame of reference in his stories is the family.

We observe the common chord tugging us ever toward the safety of womb and tomb in stories like "The Long Road to Ummera," in which an old woman values her place of burial over her earthly home, or, more clearly yet, "The Bridal Night" in which a demented young man is lulled in the night-long embrace of a Madonna-like neighbor who serves simultaneously as his wife and mother before he is put in the insane asylum. In "The Babes in the Woods," young Terry loses his benefactor-aunt because he publicly states, within the hearing of the aunt's boyfriend, what he secretly hopes: that she is his mother. In the end he is comforted by an older child, the maternal Florry:

> When she put her arms around him he fell asleep, but she solemnly remained holding him fast to her. Then she fell asleep too and didn't notice the evening train going up the valley. It was all lit up. The evenings were drawing in.

In an ending reminiscent of Joyce's "A Painful Case," the dynamic phallic train going up the valley churns on, but the peaceful child slumbers securely in Florry's fertile arms. Oblivion, a parent's reassuring arms, painless ceasing upon the midnight air, trains that carry one—usually back—from present pain: these are the regular images of O'Connor's stories. The yearning for Oedipal escape is clear in early stories such as "After Fourteen Years": "And the train took him ever farther and farther away . . . " and "The Procession of Life," in which the prostitute tells the constable: "I'm finding him a place to sleep—the poor child is perished with the cold. Leave him to me, constable. I'll look after him for the night," to later ones like "Judas": "I went to her and she hugged me and rocked me as she did when I was only a only a nipper," and "The Masculine Principle," in which a father finally finds the son he never had in the sire of his daughter's bastard. The final words of "The Grand Vizier's Daughter"—"Oh daddy, I'll never do it again! Daddy, come back to me! Come back!"—sum up the sense of lost innocence and parental longing which runs through his *oeuvre*.

O'Connor's early stories—the greatest of which is "Guests of the Nation," which I will take up shortly—have a toughness and bite, an undertone of repressed or potential violence—as in "In the Train," "The Majesty of the Law," and "The Luceys"—that he unfortunately neglected later. The stories after World War II, or at least after his fourth collection in 1947, begin to grow formulaic; many appeared in *The New Yorker* whose editors seem to have encouraged the formula. These stories often retreat from the horror and absurdity of life that one finds in his most mature stories and substitute instead puckish charm, mannered humor, quaint local color, predictable warmth, and general blandness. O'Connor grew at once too gentle—so that the successes of his later work lie mainly in slapstick, as in the Bishop of Moyle stories—and too sanguine, self-parodying, and "important," as if Yeats's warrant that he was doing for Ireland what Chekhov had done for Russia had finally begun to sink in.

What are his particular trademarks? As a young writer, O'Connor spotlights sadness and agony; constantly, he announces a text at the beginning of a story and then illustrates it fictionally. The young O'Connor hears mainly the melancholy, long withdrawing roar of life. In fact, an evocation of melancholy crowns the endings of as many stories as do those forlorn trains, and melancholy itself is the presiding humor and the omnipresent condition of consciousness, as one may easily confirm by looking into "Guests of the Nation," "Nightpiece with Figures," "After Fourteen Years," and "September Dawn," among many others. In *An Only Child*, O'Connor laments the polarity of his nature: "One of the things that I have inherited from my mother's side of the family is a passion for gaiety. I do not have it myself—I seem to take more from my father's family which was brooding, melancholy and violent. . . ." As time went on, his melancholy yielded to a more optimistic stance as his parental dependence and filial guilt waned.

O'Connor's concern with the matter of voice led to his starting stories with examples and aphorisms; he even invested several of his earlier stories with this same sort of prefatory text when he rewrote them for the collected edition of 1953. Thus, "Orpheus and His Lute" in its rewritten form starts out: "There's no music now like there used to be in the old days. People aren't as keen on it somehow." And the later version of "The Luceys" begins:

> It's extraordinary, the bitterness there can be in a town like ours between two people of the same family. I suppose living more or less in public as we do we are either killed or cured by it, and the same communal sense that will make a man be battered into a reconciliation he doesn't feel gives added importance to whatever quarrel he thinks must not be composed. God knows, most of the time you'd be more sorry for a man like that than anything else.

The familiar, expansive voice of the narrator soothes the reader as it kindles his expectations—in this sample we witness the expert attainment of O'Connor's sought-after tone of the speaking voice. It is the voice of a master storyteller—sane, unhurried, wise, amiable—a voice ridding the air between itself and the reader of all impediments. In time O'Connor elevated this device into a personal signature: "It is remarkable the difference that even one foreigner can make in a community when he is not yet accustomed to its ways. . . ." ("The Custom of the Country"); "I don't know how it is about education, but it never seemed to do anything for me but get me into trouble" ("The Idealist"); "The real trouble with love is that people want contradictory things out of it" ("The School for Wives").

O'Connor is also a fancier, as one may guess from the last paragraph, of the expanded anecdote. He told his students in the three American universities at which he taught to start their stories by finding a "theme," that is, a four-to-six line synopsis summarizing the complete story.[2] Like the stories of George Moore, O'Connor's more anecdotal stories sometimes levitate a little, contain what, in *The Lonely Voice*, he discusses under the rubric of "marvels." For example, in "The Late Henry Conran," the title character goes to America in disgrace but returns to Ireland to reclaim his "good" name after his wife refers to him in a newspaper announcement as "the late Henry Conran." That's the whole story, a terse piece of drollery about laying a ghost. In the same vein is "The Man that Stopped," which is simply about a man who, like Melville's Bartleby, prefers not to take his daily walk in any direction. Not too large a claim should be made for O'Connor as an anecdotist, but his instinct for the reader-seizing oral tone of the anecdote keeps recurring. "It was Norah Coveney, who has more queer stories than anyone in Cork, who told me this one," he starts "The Sisters," "and I have tried to retell it, so far as I could in her own words." Therein is the essence of the anecdote, the "queer story." As O'Connor wrote in his poetic epilogue to *Bones of Contention*, "From magic we come, / to magic we go."

A related habit is O'Connor's delineation of the eccentric character, usually a strong, impulsive, melodramatic, and unselfconscious person. We think of Rita in "The Mad Lomasneys," or of Ernest Thompson in "The Custom of the Country," or better yet, of Alec and Lofty in the stories to which they give their names. Lofty, a plumber, is typical: "On a job he effected the most elaborate mannerisms, rolled his dark, twinkling eyes, tugged his moustache, put on a tap he already knew to be burst and stood back to admire the results, attitudinizing with an air of profound scientific interest: sometimes he flooded a place for sheer effect." The reader never condemns O'Connor's eccentrics, and very rarely his characters at large, for they include in their ranks almost no villains.

One of the most typical and successful of O'Connor's stories, if one were to choose from among the nearly two hundred that he wrote, is "Guests of the Nation," correctly called by Brian Cleeve "in a sense the seminal story of modern Irish literature."[3] The story has as theme the centuries -old enmity between Ireland and Britain, and it is most typical of O'Connor because it illustrates the loss of fellow-feeling and basic decency that follows from the imposition of political dogma. Like several of O'Connor's early, and best, stories, "Guests of the Nation" is based on the author's personal experience, in this case on the Republican side during the Troubles. The story appeared in the January, 1931, issue of the *Atlantic Monthly* not quite two years after O'Connor sold his first short story, at a time when his reputation was local and founded mainly on a rather large handful of poems published during the 1920s.

From its opening sentence, the natural, congenial, narrative voice that was to become O'Connor's chief triumph is at work. Big and doomed Belcher shifts his legs out of the ashes "at dusk" as his fellow hostage, little 'Awkins, lights the lamp and produces the cards; the narrator and Noble join the others at the table and complete the renewed human community from whose midst division is excluded, for all four are "chums." Belcher's and 'Awkins' Englishness is in this context unimportant and accidental; the narrator assures us that he has "never seen in my short experience two men that took to the country as they did." All four are simple men, merged in the egalitarian ritual of the card-game. Two of them have low-comedy names

(Belcher's would appear later in Lucky's monologue in *Waiting for Godot*) and the Irish pair, who are in turn idealistic and gulled, are dubbed, just as comically, Noble and Bonaparte. O'Connor's prelapsarian world is violated by the assertiveness of the IRA chief, Jeremiah Donovan, an outsider, a watcher among players, a farmer among townsmen, a keeper of documents among men of imagination, a "supervisor" who "comes out with the usual rigmarole about doing our duty and obeying our superiors." What Donovan, whose name mordantly caricatures O'Connor's own and that of the great Fenian Jeremiah O'Donovan Rossa, personifies—a churlish hierarchical ideology that subverts natural impulse—will become O'Connor's object of scorn in his main stories.

Unlike the reader, the narrator, Bonaparte, fails for a time to see the execution of Belcher and 'Awkins coming, for Bonaparte is gentle and thinks that one doesn't shoot one's "chums." The author skillfully suppresses the gravity of official murder, the horror of an-eye-for-an-eye "justice" and its jolting effect on Bonaparte, until the very end. But Bonaparte's parochial mind, trained not to oppose, awakens after he tells Noble at bedtime of Donovan's intention to execute the English. The sentence, "After we had been in bed about an hour he asked me did I think we ought to tell the Englishmen," nicely hints at the discomfiture of the tossing, mulling rebels. Just when Noble and Bonaparte begin to detect that their commitment to revolution undermines their devotion to the larger pattern of human responsibility, the reader's own appreciation of the story's implications begins to grow. He sees in the running argument between the value-denouncing 'Awkins and the "Hadam and Heve"-affirming Noble a miniature of the entire British-Irish dispute, and he sees in "the old woman of the house" a varicosed Countess Cathleen full of superstitious and pagan notions about Jupiter Pluvius and how the war was started by an Italian in Japan. Deftly O'Connor moves the whole scaffold of suggestions having to do with Irish serf-mindedness, piety, matriarchy, and spiritual revolt forward to the point-zero of Bonaparte's insight into the superiority of life to politics. How affecting is Bonaparte's final realization, and how private, for here he parts company with the reflexive grief and piety of Noble and the old woman and notices what has happened in overall perspective. In doing so he posits an unwritten sequel for his life in which he will attain the widening and isolated consciousness of moral vision:

> Noble says he felt he seen everything ten times as big,
> perceiving nothing around him but the little patch of black
> bog with the two Englishmen stiffening into it; but with me
> it was the other way, as if the patch of bog where the two
> Englishmen were was a thousand miles away from me,
> and even Noble mumbling just behind me and the old
> woman and the birds and the bloody stars were all far
> away, and I was somehow very small and very lonely. And
> anything that ever happened me after I never felt the same
> about again.

One of the most trenchant conclusions to any short story since the deep and dark tarn silently closed over the House of Usher, this is a perfect exemplar of O'Connor's view of the short story as a permanently shaping moment in a character's life rather than a novelistic record of the passage of time—a view, incidentally, which grew more honored in the breach as his career continued. The feeling of loss is keen and irreversible (" . . . I never fet the same . . . again"), the sense of helplessness poignant. The external universe bears mute and eternal witness, contorted as if in pain for man's folly. The story is a glowing accomplishment for a writer still in his twenties, and it bristles with the narrator's uneducated, vernacular verve, with the patois that Kate O'Brien later saw as O'Connor's highest glory, and with the spirit of youth and vulnerability. In the rewritten version of "Guests of the Nation," the narrator becomes more of a man of the world looking back; his rough edges are gone and the original vigor is compromised by studied wisdom. The crossroads, the loss, the reshaping repudiation of "duty," the collusion with nature, the vernacular power and the even tenor of the voice, are all characteristics that O'Connor carried forward from this prototype to later stories.

The revelation that the about-to-be-shot Belcher's wife left him the handkerchief he uses as a blindfold, the letter from 'Awkins' mother that Belcher states is in 'Awkins' pocket in case his executioners want to write her, and Belcher's deference to 'Awkins who, still kicking, requires the *coup de grace* ("Give 'im 'is first. . . . I don't mind. Poor bastard, we dunno what's 'appening to 'im now.") skirt the edge of bathos. But O'Connor doesn't lose his balance. As Irish Bonaparte ties his handkerchief to that of English Belcher to complete the makeshift blindfold, an interplay of darkness and vision is set up: Bonaparte comes to participate in Belcher's death not just as a gunman but as a newly enlightened co-victim whose innocence is blasted full of holes. In Belcher's stoic, extravagant gesture lies the beginning of

Bonaparte's own disaffection and also of the courage he will need. Like the cards that were their favorite pastime, Belcher and 'Awkins go to their revenge-death as objects in a wanton game. Often O'Connor uses membership in a group—the Republican army in the first ten stories in *Guests of the Nation*, the band in "Orpheus and His Lute," the family in "The Luceys," the townspeople of Farranchreesht in "In the Train," the police in "The Majesty of the Law"—to signal the loss of individual option and impulse.

The "crossroads" ending recurs in later stories in *Guests of the Nation* (1931). In "Nightpiece with Figures," an unforgettable "young nun will not pass . . . lightly from [the] minds" of three IRA men on the run; and the appealing story "Jo" is another variation of the point of human feeling being more important than duty. Sometimes the device gets a kind of running start, with years of a person's life passing as a preliminary to an act of self-discovery. This happens, for example, in the *Bones of Contention* (1936) story "Lofty," where a short-lived humility overtakes a lifelong snob after his wife leaves him and a one-time protegé takes his place as a political force. But the most resonant use of such an ending is found in the volume's finest story, "In the Train."

Based on an actual trial O'Connor had witnessed in the Central Criminal Court in Dublin, "In the Train" is a story that only gradually comes clear. As the initial confusion—over the relation of the people in the successive train cars, the relevance of Michael O'Leary, and the nature of Helena Maguire's misdeed—slowly dissipates, the reader is heartened to discover that this story is not one of O'Connor's occasional puzzlers in which the resolution is enigmatic and yet pleased with itself: "News for the Church" and "The Sisters" leap to mind as examples of his Cheshire-Cat design. Rather, what he has done ingeniously in "In the Train" is to lift the story from its expected static setting in the courtroom and place it in the rushing train, a dynamic locale that stresses both the divisiveness of the townspeople, sitting stolidly as they are in four different cars, and also their common motion and inability to detrain until reunited again in their home-town. Union and division, independence and reliance, instinct and tribal law, are played off against one another constantly in each "smoky compartment that molted and rocked its way across Ireland."[4]

Thus, the events of the story follow "in the train" of the action at the trial where Helena was declared not guilty because the villagers lied for her, and follow also "in the train" of the enduring sentiment of country people against informing. The relations of the four separate clusters of passengers—the gentle police sergeant and his shrewish wife, the four policemen, the group of peasants, and Helena with her inebriated new acquaintance—are as automatic as the behavior of metal shavings pursuing a passing magnet. As the groups move about and interact, the private losses that prey on them slowly emerge: the sergeant's wife's failure to buy a hat in the city and the sergeant's regret at not giving her a life in the great world; the drunk's loneliness without the "sincere" Michael O'Leary; Delancey's frustrated desire to move to Waterford; climactically, Helena's loss of Cady Driscoll whom it is now too late to marry, her youth having been squandered on the boorish husband her family forced upon her. Just as her new blouse will be worn beneath her shawl, her new life will be lived in opprobrium, among the human herd now stirred up against her, like the cats who attack the policeman in Delancey's anecdote.

"The law is truly a remarkable phenomenon," the slightly "squiffy" sergeant points out to Helena; and he surely refers to the law of Farranchreest, according to which Helena will be given "the hunt" by the villagers who have controverted the formal law of the city. As they approach their own village, which seems "like the flame-black-ened ruin of some mighty city," the sergeant strikes a note of separation: "Tis time we were all getting back to our respective compartments." Temporarily forced to conform to city standards, the villagers have ignored their citizenly duty and decently lied; but for them, and so for Cady Driscoll, Helena is now a marked woman. Her life has been in decline since the judge freed her and she bought the blue blouse "on the way down from the court." At the end, confronting her own image in the train window, watching the little cottages "stepping down through wet and naked rocks to the water's edge," Helena detects that she has gone from one misfortune to a worse: "... she could only wonder at the force that had caught her up, mastered her and thrown her aside." The wording and imagery owe something to Yeats's "Leda and the Swan" and crown Helena's insight into the conflicting claims of wisdom and appetite. "In the Train" is one of O'Connor's most haunting stories. The author neatly balances the lowly and bleak life of the village and its provincial police against the bright lights of the law-affirming city and its lofty magistrates. The train of time careers along the parallel tracks of actuality and possibility.

The principal story in *Bones of Contention* after "In the Train" is "The Majesty of the Law," though "Lofty" offers a protagonist nearly as sinewy as "Majesty's" Old Dan Bride. The courtliness of Dan and the police sergeant makes "The Majesty of the Law" a masterpiece of character-drawing, a kind of verbal ballet—as "Song Without Words," about two wordless monks, is a form of mime—in which the two "dancers" keep opening their arms to catch each other. The footwork is magnificent as the crusty Dan upholds the need for law to ease the sergeant's job of arresting him, while the sergeant praises the old ways of the lawless past which Dan reverted to in opening his neighbor's head. This is O'Connor's most perfect treatment of decorum.

The thinnest and tartest of O'Connor's four volumes is *Crab Apple Jelly* (1944). Here he veers away from his origins as storyteller in the manner of Daniel Corkery and Isaac Babel and sounds the stark moral depths that so impressed him in the work of a writer to whom his mentor Corkery had introduced him—Chekhov.[5] It is Chekhov's sense of moral separation and his affirmation of life in a world of decrease that impressed O'Connor, as well as Chekhov's facility for keeping atmosphere and characterization indepedent of one another and in the most artful proportion. What O'Connor said of the great Russian applies as well to himself: "He always writes as a moralist, but his morality is no longer the morality of the group, it is the short story writer's morality of the lonely individual soul."[6] In *Crab Apple Jelly*, O'Connor's themes become the Chekhovian ones of loneliness ("Song Without Words"), aberration ("The Bridal Night"), death-yearning ("The Long Road to Ummera"), of lives wasted and opportunities missed ("Uprooted").

"The Bridal Night" is a major, brief effort, a gem. The crazed Denis's need to hold his idealized lady not only in his thoughts but in his arms abed to keep at bay the banshees of madness evokes the universally shared terror of things slipping away, of the mind's dark night. The reader concurs with Denis's aggrieved mother's remark about the sacrificial Winnie that "No one would say the bad word about her" after her night of offering Denis consolation. The temptation to scandal-mongering is thwarted by the sacramental power of human contact: "From that day to the day she left us there did no one speak a bad word about what she did.... Isn't it a strange thing and the world as wicked as it is...?" In the end, the implacable earth spins on, darkness having "fallen over the Atlantic, blank grey to its farthest reaches." The bad word of the town and the backdrop of uncaring nature mock man's pathetic liaisons, the charade of his bridal nights.

The Good Priest, based loosely on O'Connor's longtime friend

Father Tim Traylor, is a stock figure in several O'Connor stories; he makes an appearance in "'The Star That Bids the Shepherd Fold'" as the young French-speaking curate Father Devine, who, as the Good Priest often does, outsmarts—here in collusion with a German ship-captain —the agents of repression. The story is a warm-up for the more elegiac one that follows. "The Long Road to Ummera," first published in *The Bell* in October, 1940, opens with one of the loveliest paragraphs in O'Connor's work:

> Always in the evenings you saw her shuffle up the road to Miss O's for her little jobing of porter, a shapeless lump of a woman in a plaid shawl faded to the colour of snuff that dragged her head down on her bosom where she clutched its folds in one hand, a canvas apron and a pair of men's boots without laces. Her eyes were puffy and screwed up into tight little buds of flesh and her rosy old face, that might have been carved out of a turnip, was all crumpled with blindness. The old heart was failing her, and several times she would have to rest, put down the jug, lean against the wall, and lift the weight of the shawl off her head. People passed; she stared at them humbly; they saluted her; she turned her head and peered after them for minutes on end. The rhythm of life had slowed down in her till you could scarcely detect its faint and sluggish beat.

The reader cares immediately about this shuffling woman, weighted down yet determined to go her own timeless way to the end of the road. The sentences grow fragmentary and the words collapse to breathless monosyllables as her spirit flags. A dominant theme of this story, and others in *Crab Apple Jelly*, is the necessity of pride and the price one pays for self-esteem. In these stories we find O'Connor's sympathies at their widest and his style at its most suggestive and poetic—plangent and moving, yet not "melancholy." Note his closing portrait of the fields of Ummera as Abby's body is brought back to her native valley; the revolutions of life and death still trace their great circles though Abby Driscoll will go the road no more: "The lake was like a dazzle of midges; the shafts of the sun, revolving like a great millwheel, poured their great cascades of milky sunlight over the hills and the little white-washed cottages and the little black mountain cattle among the scarecrow fields."

It is not sufficiently noticed that O'Connor is a paramount social historian of a country which was leaving a static, older way of life for an acquisitive, modern one. The advent of modernism is a subject of countless Irish storytellers—from Joyce to James Plunkett and John Montague—but probably no Irish writer works the topic into the fabric of his material so implicitly yet so fully as O'Connor. His stories bridge the gap between Corkery's Munster countryside and his own Cork City and Dublin. Abby Driscoll is a typical O'Connor creation inasmuch as the stands for an older way of life as doomed and failing as she herself is; she sits in the firelight with Johnny Thornton after supper "talking about old times in the country and long-dead neighbors, ghosts, fairies, spells and charms." Meanwhile, her circumspect bourgeois son, with his grocery shop in the south Main Street and his house in Sunday's Well, has grown into "an insignificant little man" who is "jealous of the power the dead had over her." The difference between them is really not so much one of generational viewpoint as of economic values. Actually, O'Connor's well-known statement in the Foreward to the Vintage edition of his stories about his purpose in certain stories being to "describe for the first time the Irish middleclass Catholic way of life with its virtues and its faults"[7] is not a generous enough description of his social scope.

Cultural transition figures in the other principal stories in *Crab Apple Jelly*: "The Luceys," "Uprooted," and "The Mad Lomasneys." In the first, Tom and Ben Lucey carry on their sibling rivalry by remote control through their sons. Tom has long been envious of Ben's better brain, so he takes pains to provide his son Peter with an education that will guarantee Peter's social welfare; the easier-going Ben has no such anxieties about his own son, Charley, but he belittles Peter to his brother when Peter embezzles from his employer. Tom Lucey's unrelenting enmity for his brother is just as rigid and merciless as the contempt he expresses toward his son after his crime. Tom sticks to the ancient ways of spite and revenge as if they were principled: "I swore ... that never, the longest day I lived, would I take your father's hand in friendship," he tells Charley, and "I never broke my word yet, to God or man." He is probably O'Connor's chiefest eccentric, an Olympian, thought queer by the town, fond of old books, callous toward the alcoholic wife whose malady he no doubt contributed to, a hater of weakness, an opponent of the breezy slang of the day that would call a six-pence coin a "tanner." He is, in short, an anachronism, an embittered draper expecting and never getting the homage once accorded the capitalist who now must live in an egalitarian society that he detests. This is one of O'Connor's favorite strategies—to set the anachronistic character down in the midst of an updated social ambience. Usually the character fails. In "The Mad Lomasneys," Ned Lowry loses the capricious girl he loves because he is too completely a scion of the decorous Hayfield-Hourigans, too much an ancestor-worshipper, to keep up with the impulsive "chancer" Rita.

In "Uprooted," the sons are expected to compensate for the sins of the father. Old Tomas "had the gumption" and won the daughter of the O'Donnells, though they were "stiff" to him because he owned no land. To save family face, his two sons have had to go east and make something of themselves, but Ned Keating, having "fought his way through the college into a city job," is now a disappointed man. His eyes are "already beginning to lose their eagerness." He is tired of Dublin and thinks longingly of Glasgow and New York; he cannot wed the sensuous, desirable Cait, for to do so would mean going back, would mean another landless Keating buckling under to another Carriganassa heiress. By mischance Ned has spiritually uprooted himself—he cannot go home because, as he tells his brother at the end, "We made our choice a long time ago and we can't go back on it now." Ned is lost in a social time-warp, the past "outgrown" and the future "remote and intangible," another anachronism who, like Tom Lucey and Ned Lowry and many another O'Connor protagonist, is impaled on his own imperious pride.

The stories in O'Connor's fourth collection, *The Common Chord* (1948), show not a deepening sense of sympathy or of social complexity as does *Crab Apple Jelly*, but a new push by his heroes and heroines in the direction of personal freedom. Having gone through a phase of understanding their problems in *Crab Apple Jelly*, his characters now proceed to assert their independence, at least temporarily, from authority and "duty." The two opening stories in the collection are illustrative. In the first, "News for the Church," Father Cassidy humiliates the errant convent-school teacher guilty of fornication, "striping off veil after veil of romance and leaving her with nothing but a cold, sordid, cynical adventure like a bit of greasy meat on a plate." His brow-beating leads in the end to her outcry:

> "But you're making it sound so beastly," she wailed.
> "And wasn't it?" he asked with lips pursed and brows raised.
> "Ah, it wasn't, Father," she said earnestly. "Honest to God, it wasn't. At least, at the time I didn't think it was."

That carnal love can be not only pleasurable but tender is news for the Church indeed, but it fails to make a lasting impression on Cassidy, who trudges on "heavy policeman's feet" to watch the chastened girl leave "under the massive fluted columns of the portico." He is a successor of all those fierce upholders of "duty" in the early O'Connor stories, and although he has forced the girl into collapse, it is she who has taught the Church that "Honest to God, it wasn't."

The title of the second story, "The Custom of the Country," refers to the sexual inhibition of Irish womanhood. When Anna fails to convert her heathen Englishman to Irish Catholicism, she "converts" herself to heathen Englishness and, pregnant, decides to decamp for England to practice bigamy with the already married Ernest.[8] In doing so she follows the other custom of the country, that of fleeing Mammy, in whatever form Mammy may lurk. And, really, the longest and most ambitious story in *The Common Chord*, "The Holy Door," hardly differs in its central declaration. Charlie Cashman struggles to extract himself from the disagreeable control of his scorpion-like mother and his untouchable first wife. At times he has to cope with the contumely of the town and especially that of his first wife's family. But, most of all, Charlie has to free himself from his own sexual ineptness. The holy door in its primary sense refers to a consecrated place in Rome, "opened once every seven years," to which childless pilgrims go to pray for fecundity. Unabashed, O'Connor enlarges the image to include the sliding confessional door of Fr. Ring (another Good Priest), Polly's bolted bedroom door, and the ardor-arousing iron gates of life.

Full of self-doubt about his sexual prowess, Charlie is a convenient target for his mother's murderous barbs. Mrs. Cashman is one of O'Connor's last great eccentric creations. When Charlie first marries Polly, she taunts him about Polly's fallowness and, thus, his own impotency: "Many a better cake than she didn't rise." After Polly's death and Charlie's taking up with her best friend, Nora, Mrs. Cashman delivers her verdict on Nora's potential as Charlie's second wife: "That's the hand that'll never rock a cradle for you." In a frenzy of sexual anxiety, Charlie blurts out his proposition to Nora that they "have the honeymoon first and the marriage after." It is a pretty phrase but an infelicitous strategy. But the story is never allowed to slip over into farce, for Charlie's maturation gradually occurs. He sees what he really wants—the somatic Nora—and goes after her despite all opposition, including Nora's. Here is Charlie's final colloquy with the fearful Nora, the story's climax:

"But what'll you do if your mother puts spells on me?"
[Nora] asked in a dazed tone, putting her hand to her
forehead.
"Roast her over a slow fire," snapped Charlie. He was
his own man again, aged seventeen, a roaring revolutionary and rationalist, ready if necessary to take on the whole
blooming British Empire and the Catholic Church.

The cry of the independent spirit is heard in O'Connor's best
stories, capping the last stage of his growth. His early championing of
decent human contact and the deepening social understanding of his
middle years culminates in *The Common Chord*. Starting in Blarney
Lane, O'Connor ended as a citizen of the world, living now in Paris,
now in New York, comfortable in the robles of Harvard or Dublin
University, a truly "popular" writer in the best sense, one whose work
mediates between the flow of Irish writing before and after and
around even as it humanizes and entertains.

Notes

[1] Frank O'Connor, *An Only Child* (London: Macmillan, 1965) 276.
[2] See Richard T. Gill, "Frank O'Connor in Harvard," and Wallace Stegner,
"Professor O'Connor at Stanford," in *Michael/Frank: Studies on Frank O'Connor*, ed.
Maurice Sheehy (Dublin and London: Gill and Macmillan, 1969) 42 and 99.
[3] Brian Cleeve, *Dictionary of Irish Writers*(Cork: The Mercier Press, 1967) I,
101.
[4] So successful was the setting of the linked cars that, two years after the
story appeared in 1935 in *Lovat Dickson's Magazine*, O'Connor mounted a dramatic
version at the Abbey with the collaboration of Hugh Hunt.
[5] O'Connor, who staged two Chekhov plays in Cork in the late 1920s, cites
Chekhov constantly as a benchmark of quality in his writing on the theory of the
short story; *vide* his Introduction to *Modern Irish Short Stories, The Mirror in the
Roadway*, and *The Lonely Voice*.
[6] O'Connor, "The Platonist," *Michael/Frank: Studies on Frank O'Connor*, 125.
[7] O'Connor, Foreward, *Stories by Frank O'Connor* (New York: Vintage Books,
1956) vii.
[8] I give the rewritten version as it appears in the Vintage edition. In the
earlier version Anna merely takes up her pen to write Ernest without telling him to
expect her.

Chapter Three

Sean O'Faolain: Love's Old Sweet Song

I. The best commentators on O'Faolain's short story art, Maurice Harmon and Katherine Hanly,[1] have both pointed out the evolution of his writing from a romantic to a realistic mode, a course that O'Faolain himself explicitly avows in the Forward to *The Finest Stories*. To me his main development seems somewhat different. O'Faolain is the Turgenev of the modern Irish short story, a writer who gradually becomes the most continental and anti-provincial of its major practitioners after James Joyce, even though his work retains an unmistakably Irish base. His movement is from the West Corkery of *Midsummer Night Madness* and *A Purse of Coppers* to the city in his middle volumes (he has published eight volumes of new or mostly new stories). He settles down in the work of his maturity, which begins with *The Man Who Invented Sin* (1948), into a narrative voice that is more "international" than Frank O'Connor's, more reflective of *social* tableaux, the human comedy of manners, than that of any other major Irish short story writer.

A few words on influences are necessary. If O'Connor flows out of George Moore—ultimately out the *shanachie's* country art and anecdotalism—O'Faolain's model has been Joyce with his strong formal, "literary," and city ways.[2] The resemblances to *Dubliners* in O'Faolain's work are so manifold as to outweigh his and Joyce's two most obvious differences: Joyce's persistent reliance on symbolism (O'Faolain's penchant is for a suggestive method that runs oblique to symbolism, as we shall see), and Joyce's persistent theme of paralysis (O'Faolain's view, which he sometimes departs from, is of the Irish nation as sleeping but not spiritually dead).[3]

To Frank O'Connor, his tutor and fellow Corkonian Daniel Corkery remained a warm friend and active influence over his lifetime; in O'Faolain's case, Corkery's influence is to be found only in his earliest volume, *Midsummer Night Madness*, and Corkery the man gradually became viewed by O'Faolain, as we see in *Vive Moi!*, as a provincial who "had never been to any university and had no degree whatever,"[4] a rival who inexplicably won the chair of English at University College Cork from O'Faolain who had studied languages and literatures at two universities. It is to the city that O'Faolain characteristically turned, away from the political, mythical, and local life of Corkery's peasantry and toward the social implications of the city seen (as in Joyce) as a microcosm of the world. The preoccupations and institutions of middle-class urban society—courtship, marriage, job, acquisition and "success," adultery, selfness in the midst of the swarm; in short, social and domestic stability and the breaches thereof— were to become his stocks-in-trade.

Even in his earliest stories, O'Faolain saw the agrarian past sadly but inevitably on the wane. In the title story of his first volume, the gorgeously overdone *Midsummer Night Madness*, the great house of Old Henn, threatened with arson by the revolutionary lout Stevey Long, is a last vestige of the romantic Ireland that is dead or going. Henn proceeds to Paris at the end, while the narrator, a city boy denounced by Stevey and his gang of bullies, retains his somewhat stuffy integrity. In a later story in the volume, "The Small Lady," a monastery replaces the great house as an emblem of the dying social order—the monastery is now a sometime refuge for alcoholics who are presided over by a run-down priest. (I will return to both of these highly interesting stories later.) Increasingly, O'Faolain deserts the countryside, though never the out-of-doors, and moves toward the ambience of the city. Thus John Chamberlain in 1932 called *Midsummer Night Madness* the most worthy successor to date of *Dubliners*,[5] and Maurice Harmon found in O'Faolain a resolution of the Joycean quandry: " ... his work is an interesting example of how an artist stays and faces up to home, fatherland, and church."[6]

From the beginning the influence of Joyce keeps cropping up in O'Faolain. The last sentence of the early story "A Broken World" makes one think of Gabriel Conroy listening to the tap-tap of the flakes on the window of the Gresham: "In the morning, Ireland, under its snow, would be silent as a perpetual dawn." A "quincunx" of stars appears in "Admiring the Scenery," the same odd word that Joyce uses in "Grace." The plot line of "A Born Genius" in which Pat Linehan can not bring himself to leave Cork for a fuller life is precisely that of "Eveline," while Ike Dignam, in "Persecution Mania," mirrors the hair-trigger litigiousness of Dennis Breen in *Ulysses* after Ike receives a suggestive but anonymous postcard. Benjie, in "Childybawn," thinks his mother "ought to be put in the Budget," an Irishism that Mollie

Bloom uses to capture the sense of wonder that her husband's arcane proposals arouse in her. (Mollie Bloom is mentioned by the hero of O'Faolain's "The Faithless Wife" as the single real woman in the Irish novel, though he later reforms his view of her as being only "James Joyce in drag.") In "Angels and Ministers of Grace," the bed-ridden Jackie Neason quixotically consumes the *Catholic Encyclopedia*, a mental ingestion that leads him into raging theological arguments; from the title onward one is prompted to think of Tom Kernan's bedroom battlefield in "Grace." And the hesitant nature of the love-affair in "The Inside Outside Complex" with its anxious (but frozen) superannuated lovers brings "A Painful Case" immediately to mind.

As with O'Connor, the successive titles of O'Faolain's short story volumes depict the direction of his career, one that widens slowly to wisdom and faith in life. The naivety of his life's "midsummer" gives way in *A Purse of Coppers* (1937) to his rejection of his materialistic countrymen who fumble in the greasy till. Lost innocence and an encroaching awareness of evil is next in *The Man Who Invented Sin* (1949), before he composes his version of *À la recherche du Temps Perdu* in *I Remember! I Remember!* (1961). In this last-mentioned volume, O'Faolain launches into his major theme of nostalgia and examines the effects of desire and random chance upon memory. Passion becomes a main emphasis beginning with *The Heat of the Sun* (1969), the writing of which corresponds in time with its author's developing affection for Italy, the country he has written about more than any place except Ireland. Finally, *The Talking Trees* (1970) and *Foreign Affairs* (1975) reflect an expanding imaginative understanding. "Talking trees" evoke the bird-filled and sacred wood of O'Faolain's secular imagination—his point of widest empathy. Thereafter, the "foreignness" of his most recent title suggests the expanding focus of his settings, his internationalism.[7]

If it is so that O'Faolain came out from under Joyce's overcoat— to paraphrase Turgenev's remark about Gogol—then one may ask what distinguishes him from O'Connor. Surely they started out similarly: the first important story of each evokes the torment of the Civil War period, though "Midsummer Night Madness" sprawls and dawdles more than "Guests of the Nation." Fundamentally, it seems to me that O'Faolain's work grows in quality and strength over the course of his writing life, while O'Connor's declines in merit in late mid-career after his fourth volume in 1947. Somehow O'Faolain's education and mixed experience and his excursions into other *genres* of writing in his middle years helped him to stretch his view of life and to learn to vary his techniques; this is not true of O'Connor who approaches perfection in his narrow, deep *metier* but lacks the talent or inclination to goad himself beyond that.

There are times within a few stories when frankly I can not tell the writing of one from that of the other, but those occasions occur only when I am reading their earlier and lesser-known works. The best stories of O'Faolain—"In the Bosom of the Country," "Lovers of the Lake," "Up the Bare Stairs," "The Sugawn Chair," "Dividends," "The Silence of the Valley," "The Faithless Wife"—are surely equalled by the best stories of O'Connor—"Guests of the Nation," "In the Train," "The Majesty of the Law," "The Luceys," "The Holy Door," "The Custom of the Country," "Uprooted." But over the long haul O'Connor grows mannered and constricted, even repetitious. O'Faolain's well-known comment on O'Connor's inexactness is exact: "He was like a man who takes a machine-gun to a shooting gallery. Everybody falls flat on his face, the proprietor at once takes to the hills, and when it is all over, and you cautiously peep up, you find that he has wrecked the place but got three perfect bull's-eyes."[8] O'Connor is everywhere caught in the oral story-teller's bind which encourages subjectivism and the repetition of known elements of plot and embellishment. O'Faolain's stories broaden out toward ever-larger perceptions of human manners. John V. Kelleher observed this maturation in 1957 when he described O'Faolain as "no longer distracted by Ireland" but having more verve and humor, a sharper sense of judgment, than in his earlier stories.[9]

O'Connor can be funnier; Lavin more insightful of social nuance, more "Jamesian"; O'Flaherty more elemental, hard-edged, and painterly. But O'Faolain's work stands at the cumulative center of the Irish short story, the apogee of the form. His narrative voice is always just a bit, but artfully, disingenuous, curious, unshowy, restrained, knowing. O'Connor, whose single, constant narrator and whose characters read minds too clairvoyantly, is never quite as believable, just as his wonderful but steamrolling eccentrics are exaggerated compared to O'Faolain's. Think of Aunty Anna in "Dividends" in contrast to Rita Lomasney, for example, or of two opinionated male converts absorbing the astonishing dogmas of Catholicism, Major Frank Keene in O'Faolain's "In the Bosom of the Country" and Ernest Thompson in O'Connor's "The Custom of the Country": O'Faolain's habit is to underplay his effects, to let his characters adjust as they detect the complexity of things, while O'Connor's method is more monochromatically a "send-up."

Sometimes the reader's settled view of an O'Faolain character or a plot is forced to alter—an unexpected hero, lying in wait, emerges as the story takes on broader implications. This happens from the beginning of his canon. In "Midsummer Night Madness," John, the young narrator, learns sympathy for the Anglo-Irishman Henn whose natural dignity is that of "a Hapsburg or a Bourbon." John sees the knottiness of class roles and the fraudulence of class stereotypes in Irish life—the real fools are John's fellow-revolutionaries who would write off Protestants like Old Henn. Similarly, in "Lord and Master," Lord Carew ends up winning the reader's respect and the chauvinistic schoolmaster turns out to be selfish and petty.

The apparent point may not turn out to be *the* point in O'Faolain; life is rich and mysterious, he keeps indicating, neat answers are like quicksilver. The promiscuous Mrs. Sidney Browne, the putative villain of "The Small Lady," takes on an affecting courage and resolution when she writes her last letter before being executed. Not only the unexpected but the ambivalent is a natural part of O'Faolain's outlook. The red-headed Scottish girl in "The Silence of the Valley" who is "on a hair trigger between a glowering Beethoven and *The Laughing Cavalier*" neatly personifies the complicated poles of the story which deal with the old ways of the valley that are now giving way to "progress." "Yes," she states with "sheer joy" in the story's final words, "it will be another grand day—tomorrow." But immediately "her eyebrows sank, very slowly, like a falling curtain." We doubt that it will or can be.

The point is that part of O'Faolain's success lies in his ability to transmit a perpetual feeling of wonder, to present his tales as conjectures about the many-sidedness of things, as speculations on a social complex of the sort that intrigued Flaubert, Balzac, and James. Conjecture and ambivalence vivify such stories as "Admiring the Scenery," "The Man Who Invented Sin," "Teresa," "Up the Bare Stairs," "Lovers of the Lake," and, most triumphantly, "Dividends." In his Foreward to *The Finest Stories*, O'Faolain reviews the effects on his literary style of deliberately alternating romantic and realistic phases in a vocabulary of value-system terms. The consummation of the whole blend, he feels, has been ambivalence: "This ambivalence, once perceived, demanded a totally new approach. I have been trying to define it ever since." The ambivalence or "totally new approach" runs sometimes close to the riddle, sometimes to allegory. As O'Faolain employs them, both methods bespeak not indecisiveness on his part but rather his overall belief that human happiness is thwarted—on the personal level by ego and solipsism and on the social level by taboo and institutional *fiat*. One pursues happiness, expecting nothing from it but elusiveness.

The ending of "Lovers of the Lake" is an example of an O'Faolain riddle. For the entire day after leaving the religious retreat at Lough Derg together, the Grania-and-Diarmuid-like lovers sharpen their sensual appetites tantalizingly. They are "love-drunk," trembling with anticipation. They draw apart on the promenade of the hotel after a final passionate kiss: "She knew what that kiss implied. Their mouths parted. Hand in hand they walked slowly back to the hotel, to their separate rooms." The passion of the kiss *should* imply the signaling of sexual acquiescence, for after all Jenny and Bobby have just indulged their other appetites to satiety in wine, food, and music until they are "Gently tipsy, gently tired." But Bobby's chance remark, meant to win Jenny's favor, that he wouldn't mind going on the retreat again a year later when "I might do it properly," causes a reaction of bittersweet resistance in Jenny—for him, she sees, the retreat has been mainly a generous tactic in his campaign to reconquer her. "Not tonight," she tells him. But will it be any night? Can the bold lover ever do more than kiss? What is important is that O'Faolain has made us *care* about the lovers, despite the unclear outcome of their affair. Their complex emotions are unselfish and far-reaching. Somehow, in the end, the riddle of the story's ending widens the reader's sympathies for the two characters. O'Faolain accepts George Eliot's *dictum* that "If art does not enlarge men's sympathies it does nothing morally." We consistently end up caring for his characters, despite O'Faolain's occasional inconclusive plot resolutions and ambivalent character motivations.[11]

Just one more example of the riddle technique. At the end of "The Old Master," a story about a pompous but likeable blowhard who bends his principles when challenged by clerical disapproval, O'Faolain leaves us with this question: should John Aloysius Gonzago O'Sullivan have sacrificed his sinecure and his highly popular niche as a town buffoon in order to become a spurned man of consequence? "I wonder if there is any wrong or right in that [question]?" O'Faolain winds up, "Or is it, as John would have said, that one kind of life is just the same as another in the end?" Who can say? We can only attest to the myriadness of forces that misshaped John from the start, and to life's chanciness. One is reminded of the doleful Hanafan's query in a slightly later story, "Admiring the Scenery": "I wonder . . . do the common people ever admire scenery?" To do so becomes in the course of the story synonymous with living out one's conception of oneself, that is, with the same quandary that confronted O'Sullivan in "The Old Master." Something has made Hanafan a sour man—how might it have been different? Along with O'Faolain we are made to wonder. "To which of these men had she given herself?" he asks about the pregnant Gypsy at the end of "Midsummer Night Madness"—to Henn, who is about to marry her, or to Stevey Long, who made her pregnant, the old or the new Ireland? The question being asked really is, where is Ireland going from here? Like Yeats, O'Faolain likes questions more than answers.

O'Faolain's penchant for a method on the fringe of allegory achieves its crowning outlet in "A Broken World," "Admiring the Scenery," "A Born Genius," "Discord," "Mother Matilda's Book," and, better yet, "The Man Who Invented Sin," "The Fur Coat," and "The End of a Good Man." The first five of these stories use a traditional allegorical method rather self-consciously, though not with a heavy hand: men's occupations and predispositions stand for entire classes and viewpoints, settings suggest ideas and values, moments are epicenters of eternity. In O'Faolain's mature work, which I would date from the end of World War II, his allegorical method gains in drollery and cleverness. There is a new, gently mocking satire, and the darting bite of irony.

Surely these qualities are what illuminate "The Man Who Invented Sin" in which Old Nick himself appears in the disarming guise of the youthful curate called Lispeen (Irish for frog, one of the forms assumed by the deteriorating Satan). Lispeen despoils the innocence of the four vacationing monks and nuns, making them feel dirty to such an extent that a life-long pall is thrown over their innate joy. When the narrator encounters Father Lispeen twenty years later, he is "scarcely changed" except that he now cuts a Fred Astair-like swath, flaunting "a tall silk hat and . . . a silver-headed umbrella." He laughs, as the narrator says, "so merrily at the memory of those old days that I almost expected him to clap me on the back." His rubicund face glows and shines. How charming O'Faolain's picture of evil is, and how conciliatory Lispeen's pastoral declaration that the four religious were "Such innocents!. . . . Of course, I *had* to frighten them!" Lispeen prances off at the end, hearty and beaming reassurance, emitting a final heigh-ho as "his elongated shadow waved behind him like a tail." The story, like its title, is first-rate. The dandified devil's ironic mission is not to prompt the innocent occupants of Mrs. Tyler's garden to sin, as one might expect, but to cause them to find their joyful natures repulsive.

"The Fur Coat" and "The End of a Good Man" reflect the same kind of witty and wise allegory. In the former—a popular anthology piece—the middle-aged couple who have arrived at a state of comfortable means and want to indicate their success to the world by garbing the wife in an expensive coat, are prevented from doing so by their own ineradicable past. People—especially decent Irish serf-minded people—can not, O'Faolain demonstrates, "sin" against such life-long habits as frugality. The coat is more than a mantle of class position; to buy it means that the Maguires must repudiate their foregoing lives as revolutionaries and sacrificing patriots. Molly's old coat is an irreplaceable flag of materialistic indifference. The story may well refer to O'Faolain's personal life at the time, for it shows its author wondering what trophies of success he might not hope for now that a more than national reputation had been bestowed upon him.

In the other story, "The End of a Good Man," Larry Dunne's racing pigeon Brian Boru is defeated by Michael Collins the Second: past heroism's replacement by present vulgar opportunism is a persistent viewpoint of O'Faolain who opposed Collins' Free Staters in the Civil War. Larry himself sees the bird and its flight in allegorical terms as he describes his winless champion stranded on a telegraph pole: "Isn't that poor Ireland all over again? First in the race. Fast as the lightning. But she won't settle down! That bird has too much spirit— he's a high-flier—and sure aren't we the same? Always up in the bloody air. Can't come down to earth." Larry kills the thing he loves most with an IRA pistol, has the bird stuffed "and put in the window of his lane cabin for the world to see." Here is O'Faolain's repeated theme that he who chooses to live strictly by the past will perish by the past. Poor rusticated Larry becomes like a stuffed owl, memorizing Who's Who, gazing into the fire while the pigeon's eyes stare glassily out at the bloody sky, both of them grounded high-fliers.

"The Man Who Invented Sin" appeared first in The Bell in December, 1944, just after O'Faolain had published in the same magazine a series of five pedestrian articles on "The Craft of the Short Story." With "Teresa" the story signals O'Faolain's deepening emotional understanding and artistic control during this period. His style is now stripped of indulgences, and the material is presented more objectively by a more detached narrator who looms nearby fixing the values by which the story is to be apprehended. From "Mother Matilda's Book," written a short time before "The Man Who Invented Sin," to "Up the Bare Stairs," written shortly thereafter, O'Faolain settled into a method that incorporated Henry James's habit of immersion in "felt life" and of subtle technical effects with Somerset Maugham's masterful story-telling sense. "Mother Matilda's Book," about a mad old nun assigned to write the history of her order who includes all the shocking gossip of the neighborhood, is a model of droll social satire and allegorical suggestiveness. "Up the Bare Stairs" has its own fringe-allegory, as the title indicates: Francis James Nugent, the newly created baronet who is taking his mother's corpse home to Cork, has fought his way up in the world. His success has been achieved spitefully, in order to teach his parents and teacher a lesson. The title of the story also calls to mind the outcast Dante, lonely in exile, dependent on the generosity of others. In both "Teresa" and "Up the Bare Stairs," one can see very clearly O'Faolain's improving skill in developing character through dialogue; previously he had had to resort to often ponderous exposition.

Linked to O'Faolain's sense of wonder and allegorizing habit in his mature work is his continual refinement of the quality of sentiment, sentiment related to the Romantic trait of sensibility. In O'Faolain sentiment is frequently in the company of its first cousin, nostalgia, in a comedy-of-manners setting. Sentiment informs O'Faolain's middle-aged (and older) characters who by the mid-1940's become his customary *personae*. It is true that he later wrote of children here and there, as in "The Talking Trees," but only rarely and not in the sentimental manner of O'Connor. Sentiment is a perquisite of age in O'Faolain, as we readily notice in stories like "The Sugawn Chair," "Two of a Kind," "In the Bosom of the Country," "Dividends," and "The Faithless Wife." As social comedies the last three are not only strongly Jamesian; they are worthy of James. A word on each of the five will help illustrate O'Faolain's characteristic use of feeling, sentiment, and nostalgia.

"The Sugawn Chair" is a gem. Barely three pages long, it describes the efforts of the narrator's parents to restore an old chair which reminds them of their growing old, of their lost country origins, and of their early love for one another. The father's inability to repair the seat of the chair with new rush affirms that the family's removal to the city is irreversible. The feeling of secure affection, child for parents and parents for one another, is perfectly and beautifully caught. Here is the final sentence, which tells of the now-grown narrator coming upon the skeleton of the chair in cleaning out the attic after his parents' deaths: "As I looked at it I smelled apples, and the musk of Limerick's dust, and the turf-tang from its cottages, and the mallows among the limestone ruins, and I saw my mother and father again as they were that morning—standing over the autumn sack, their arms about one another, laughing foolishly, and madly in love again."

In addition to extolling the saving power of memory, O'Faolain sometimes promotes new relationships for people whose youth has faded. In "Two of a Kind," the lonely merchant sailor and his neglected aunt in Brooklyn spin out wonderful lies to one another about the joy of their lives since leaving Ireland, but the lies collapse as their filial and maternal affection grows. The emphatic sentiment of the story is centered on the couple's terrible aloneness in the midst of hordes. With "The Sugawn Chair," it is one of O'Faolain's best heart-twisters. "In the Bosom of the Country" is likewise energized by engrossing sentiment, largely because of the presence in it of three transcendently well-drawn characters. The most interesting is the retired British army major, Frank Keene, who marries Anna Mohun six months after her alcoholic husband's death. Frank, who has converted to Roman Catholicism under the tutelage of the admirable local monsignor in order to please Anna, discovers with a shock that her religion is at best vestigial and perfunctory while his has become so intense that it borders on fanaticism. After the death of the monsignor, his religious frenzy abates like a fever breaking, and the couple in the end leaves "the bosom of the country" to live in a state of spiritual limbo on the continent. O'Faolain's sentiment is directed at showing the contest between religion and the desire for human perfection—the monsignor and Frank have become too saintly to survive in a hazy spiritual environment that is not equal to their purity of spirit. Ironically, Anna is quite totally bereft of sentiment.

From a plangent religious environment O'Faolain moved to an insensitive business environment in one of his very best stories, "Dividends." The business viewpoint is personified in Mel Meldrum, stock-broker of Cork, who is reluctant to prolong a harmless conspiracy with the narrator Sean to delude Sean's slightly dotty aunt, Anna Maria Whalen, into believing that she is still entitled to her "divvies" on shares that she sold months before. The prevailing sentiment in operation here is pity; as Sean says of Mel Meldrum: "I . . . wondered a little how such a man could see nothing wrong with giving charity outside his office in the name of St. Vincent de Paul but everything wrong with the idea of bestowing largesse inside it in the name of pity." Needless to say, Mel's hard commercial veneer is softened in the course of the story, chiefly by the patrician aunt and Mel's lovely cook-typist-inamorata Sheila to whom he resists proposing. Good women wear down his priggishness and teach him to follow his own *dictum* that he who doesn't speculate can't accumulate. Mel learns pity, cuts off the compromising situation with Sheila, and replaces her in his kitchen with, of all people, Aunt Anna, who upon her death bequeaths her non-existent dividends to him.

In addition to pity, the two women teach Mel generosity, duty, and sacrifice. But principally Mel's instructress is old Aunt Anna: elderly wisdom is a commonplace in O'Faolain, even more so than in other Irish writers. "Youth only knows embryos," Sean muses, for wisdom comes late: " . . . we do all the important things of life for reasons . . . of which reason knows nothing—until about twenty years after." The French diplomat, Ferdinand Louis Jean-Honoré Clichy (!), who pursues the title character in "The Faithless Wife," likewise achieves understanding only in later life when he has been transferred from Brussels to Los Angeles. The Irish, he attests, "whether as wives or mistresses . . . are absolutely faithless." The story throbs with a delicate, wistful sentiment, mainly inspired by Ferdy's passionate but temporary enchantment with the lovely Mrs. O'Sullivan in this so-phisticated boudoir comedy.

Several of the sentiment-laden stories just referred to are from O'Faolain's sixth volume of short stories, *The Heat of the Sun*, the title of which is taken from the moody song in Shakespeare's *Cymbeline*, "Fear no more the heat of the sun, / Nor the furious winter's rages. . . ." The stanza ends with the well-known fatalistic statement about golden lads and lasses coming to dust. Over and over O'Faolain tells the story of the bittersweet period of life in middle-age when human passion burns not hottest but most impulsively and desper-ately. The topic of his best work is, in two words, mature love, and one has to go to the literary pantheon—to Balzac, Stendhal, Tolstoy, and George Eliot—to locate his equals in this vein. In sum, O'Faolain's usual narrative voice is that of a *sec*, sentimental, ironic sensibility speculating archly upon the matings and mismatings in the domestic arena.

His combination of dry wit and rich feeling is perhaps exempli-fied best in the late story, "The Inside Outside Complex," in which the middle-aged lovers watch the odd menage they compose through a mirror that has been placed outside their livingroom window. Thus they end up where they started in their youth, as watchers. Ideal love and the vanity of youthful wishes are tenderly mocked in this story and elsewhere in O'Faolain by people too sensible and too scarred for idealism yet always ready to be reawakened. Bertie Bolger's van driver, who unobtrusively decamps at the end of "The Inside Outside Complex" after delivering the mirror, takes with him without knowing it the shade of Maisie Benson's dead husband, leaving the bizarre couple to start their largely-over lives together in the afterglow of their reflected image. "We'll leave it there always!," Bertie says of the mirror outside their livingroom window. "'It makes everything more real!' At which, as well she might, she burst into laughter at the sight of him staring out at himself staring in.... She had heard country tales about people who have seen on the surface of a well, not their own hungry eyes but the staring eyes of love." In this bittersweet inversion of Joyce's "A Painful Case," the voyeur-lover gets the girl rather than ossifying with fright.

In general, then, it seems true that O'Faolain is an idealistic writer like Frank O'Connor, but that O'Connor's optimism is more naive and puckish while O'Faolain's stories persistently emit a miasma of hope. O'Faolain's work reflects the spirit that Lionel Trilling correlated with the liberal imagination. His stories celebrate good food and good drink, friendship, fireplaces, and intimate conversations over brandy and do it without false heartiness. It is possible to see the food and drink as sublimations of sexual activity which O'Faolain does not describe and which the short story, directed throughout its heyday at family audiences, has hardly ever described. His stories illustrate not only loyalty to friends but to his sense of place as an Irishman, a patriotism conceived in large terms and modified by an intelligent man's misgivings. His fight against censorship and narrow nationalism during his years as editor of The Bell is well known, yet he stands outside the great expatriate tradition of Irish writers of his century from Moore and Joyce to O'Casey and Beckett. For the most part his transplanted Irish characters, who crop up more plentifully as his career progresses, either yearn for Ireland, as in "Two of a Kind" and "Teresa," or actually set out to return to it, as in "Before the Day Star."

The day star, and the north star, and the evening star, incidentally, figure regularly in O'Faolain's stories—in "Midsummer Night

Madness," "The Small Lady," "Before the Day Star," "Admiring the
Scenery," "Teresa," and "Lord and Master," for instance, though there
are more—and suggest, always, hope: a sense of direction sublimally
detectable in the rioting skies. In fact, in the earlier stories nature in
general is rhapsodized upon, but it is soon nudged aside by a greater
interest in character analysis. Liam O'Flaherty's sort of nature—
nature as impersonal biological process—has never interested O'Faolain, as anyone who reads O'Faolain's "The Trout," which reflects its
author's discomfort with O'Flaherty's customary subject matter, will
quickly notice.

No pun is intended in saying that O'Faolain, like O'Connor, is
at his worst when dealing with evil. With the exception of "The Man
Who Invented Sin," in which the devil is caricatured, he prefers to deal
with malice, overweening ambition, class-arrogance, ancestor-
worship, insincerity and infidelity in friendship and marriage—with
social aberration and bad manners rather than with mortal sin. Which
is not to say that his overall *bonhomie* is ever disingenuous.

I turn now to examining eleven of O'Faolain's most typical
stories, written over the course of his career, in order to see at closer
hand his technique and development.

II. O'Faolain's early stories, that is, those in his first two
volumes *Midsummer Night Madness* (1932) and *A Purse of Coppers*
(1938), reflect a picture of Ireland in the Twenties in a state of devolu-
tion— a confused and fragmented body-politic plunging into a deep
sleep. For a person who served for years in the Irish Volunteers, the
IRA, and the Irish Irregulars, O'Faolain as a young writer was curi-
ously uncommitted to political positions. The overall statement of his
first two bodies of stories is a conservative one, namely that the
political ferment of 1916-23 crippled the old order of aristocracy and
church, while the expected land reforms that should have ensued with
Free State status were thwarted by a general despondency under
Cosgrave and by the shifting of an agrarian population to the cities
and towns.

The seven stories in *Midsummer Night Madness* deal with the
Troubles—thus O'Faolain looked back ten years for the material of this
volume, years that he had spent mostly outside of Ireland. The two
stories that typify the collection in subject matter while demonstrating

his best early manner are the title story and "The Small Lady." They are both fairly long efforts, full of the lushness of phrase that O'Faolain later muted out. They are often quite labored. The plot of the title story, which comes first in the collection, has already been adumbrated; "The Small Lady" is placed sixth and the volume as a whole has, like *Dubliners*, a pattern of organic continuity—thus, in the final story, "The Death of Stevey Long," poetic justice exerts itself when Long, the callow villain of story number one, is tried and executed for the murder of Mother Dale, the protagonist of the third story, "The Bombshop." The reader writhes in discomfort when the IRA buries the miserable Stevey with full military honors. But though unworthy of public homage, he was actually innocent of Mother Dale's death. O'Faolain is an accurate social chronicler as he depicts with heavy irony the confusion and myopia of all the political viewpoints of the period.

The most powerful single image of Old Henn in "Midsummer Night Madness" is of him dragged from sleep, besotted and bedraggled, by the narrator and Henn's waiting-girl Gypsy. He sits up in bed framed against the fire that Stevey Long has set at the big house of the Blakes across the valley, "like a picture of Juan in hell." Henn is a titan, still at eighty more of a man than Stevey will ever be, a self-described "colonialist" of Irish land and women who believes his own exaggerations about the good that his ancestors and class have done for the country. He sits in a drunken stupor before the fireplace, playing resoundingly a British recording of *Don Giovanni*, as unrepenting as the impious rake of Moliere and Mozart. Henn has what Yeats called "the pride of the people that were bound neither to Cause nor to State." His first reaction to the burning out of the Blakes is to think of the rooks in their roof: "They'll never nest there again. They're ruined with the heat." Henn is pathetic, noble, demented, a natural force. All of his larger-than-life qualities break with wonder upon the young narrator from the city who has never before seen a member of the Ascendency class near-to-hand. His response is unabashed admiration. Henn is a representative Anglo-Irishman in character and fate: old and used up, he stands in parallel to his shotgun bride, the tinker Gypsy, also a member of an ancient and disenfranchized minority that by legend descends from the Wild Geese. Henn, "in a palsy of trembling, dragging his nightshirt over his head, rump-naked, fumbling for his clothes by the pale light of the candle and the fluttering light of the burning house," sums up the plight of his class.

He is a touching comedown from the old, fierce Henn who once chased John's mother in his pelt when she was a girl and cut across his field.

Henn's big red house is a fit size for a revolutionist's *Walpurgis-nacht*. To save it from arson, he acquiesces to Stevey's demand that he marry Gypsy who is carrying Stevey's child. To Stevey, Henn is "an English pimp"; to John and the reader, he is a dissolute gentleman who befriends the coarse tinker wench when Stevey will not, just as he takes in the stunned Blakes though " they'd rather die than come under my roof." In a beautiful valetudinarian gesture, Henn sweeps out of the story with Gypsy, still proud, mischievously boasting that "if it's a boy, 'twill keep the name alive." To John—who is transparently John Whalen from Half Moon Street, Cork—he is like "a Hapsburg or a Bourbon." O'Faolain becomes enmeshed in Henn's perverse character and circumvents the conventional political or economic moral which the story seemed at first to intend having. O'Faolain's preference for life over politics is made emphatic as well in other places in *Midsummer Night Madness*, for instance in the fourth story, "The Patriot," where the honeymooning hero turns away fom his old mentor, the tub-thumping crusader of the title, to his wife's body. Likewise, in "The Small Lady," the same preference is educible.

The title character, Mrs. Sidney Browne, is a feminine counterpart of Old Henn. She is the wife of a British colonial officer ("Jack"— that is, John Bull) presently posted to India. Her penchant is to strip off her clothes and stand naked to the rain and moonlight—it is in this state that she first seduces the university student, Denis, who is assigned to guard her. To her intimates (a sizeable group), the small lady is known as Bella, a name that suggests her war-likeness and her beauty, as Denis' suggests his latent associations with Dionysius. Though she has informed on six IRA men and is about to be executed for it, the lady is not political but purely physical, a demiurge, a spectral, insatiable Lamia—in Denis' view she is Hesperus, the evening star, whose other name is Venus. After her death and Denis' escape from the pursuing Tans, he comes back down to earth in a place and mood of gaiety and rejoicing with his friend Rory, a valley where "it was another world."[12]

Bella's loss of life and divestiture of the garments of rank in "The Small Lady" equate with Old Henn's loss of country and finery: to O'Faolain their death and expulsion subtract from what little the country has of vividness and style. Denis-Sean drops into his private valley of youthful promise, but the rest that remains in the land is moribund: a run-down monastery, mute priests, a deserted chapel, a puritanical constable who informs to the Tans (he is, in fact, Denis' own father). This and other early stories offer a country in the act of extirpating its color and definition; those qualities would return to O'Faolain's stories in the 1950's after three decades of national greyness, when the modern Irish nation emerged as a backdrop for his best work.

Another story which shows O'Faolain's early misgivings about the state of Ireland is "A Broken World," which sets the tone for his second collection, *A Purse of Coppers*(1938). This story takes place on a train heading eastward to, probably, Dublin and reports the opinions on his homeland of an outspoken priest and the non-reaction to them of a phlegmatic farmer. Each departs from the train at his own stop and in bad humor; the narrator is left to his musings as the train makes its final run into the snowy city. The setting of the story suggests O'Connor's "In The Train," the technique of which we know O'Faolain held in high regard.[13] As in O'Connor's story, the train represents process, the ongoing action of life grinding along through time. The crabbed, "hellish" priest must, by force of nature, speak his piece on the subject of higher unity before he has to depart the scene, while the torpid farmer, associated with "all that belongs to the first human that was ever made," must stumble out of the train "exactly like an old black mongrel loping home." Like Old Henn and Bella Browne, they are two anachronisms who have had their chance in turn, the man of the spirit and the man of the flesh, past idealism and present sloth, one all fiery opinion, the other all watery fecklessness. They are unappealing not only to the narrator and reader but to one another, the last tired expression of theocracy and rustic grandeur. Just as dubious is the fate of the narrator who gets off at *his* stop, the snowy city. He thinks: "three bits of separateness, the priest, the farmer, and myself, flung off [the train] like bits of the *disjecta membra* of the wheel of life." The troubled narrator poses the question with which the grim allegory concludes: what rough beast can be expected in the future?, "what image . . . could warm" the people as the old religion once did, "what image of life . . . would fire and fuse us all . . . "? The story ends with the snow over everything and the train chugging off.

"A Broken World" contributes to one's feeling that the fourteen stories in *A Purse of Coppers* were low tide for O'Faolain's confidence and art. The pure depression of the story, its final jeremiad that "under

that white shroud covering the whole of Ireland, life was lying broken
and hardly breathing," shows the extent of O'Faolain's emergence
from the provincial influence of Corkery whose work had warmed his
early days. Instead he now reflects the jaundiced viewpoint of his new
mentor, Edward Garnett, toward the artistic life of Ireland.[14] The
priest's history of his mountainy parish in Wicklow where he served
when first ordained is really the history of Ireland to O'Faolain's day—
the tribes, the "foreign" names coming in, the military deployments of
'98, the perpetual sub-dividing of the land by the indigenous population while the baronial families married only among themselves, the
emigrations, the serf-mindedness, the land deserted by people gone to
"live in the towns and the cities and work for wages." The gentry have
been driven out, or reduced to rubble, while the Church and the
farmers have grown disaffected with one another; the snow is general
all over Ireland. Desperately, O'Faolain asks the question that follows
in the wake of Joyce's "The Dead": what hope is there for the future?
O'Faolain's tentative reply is to be found in "Admiring the Scenery." It
involves making a separate peace in one's imagination.

Clearly, O'Faolain's perplexities and despondencies at the time
of writing *A Purse of Coppers* are the problems of a no-longer-young
writer sorting out his prospects and liabilities. The persistence of the
"riddle" format at this time suggests his tentativeness. His artistic
psyche was suspended between the lush bathos of his first volume and
the later smooth and worldly veneer. During the later Thirties, he was
newly back from several years of living in America and England and
fighting for a toehold as a writer in Ireland. He wrote thirteen separate
volumes during the decade of the Thirties, including four biographies,
three novels, a translation of lyric poetry, and a play for the Abbey
Theatre. "Admiring the Scenery" gives an insight into the feeling of
unsettledness in his total outlook, of being betwixt-and-between.

Like "A Broken World," "Admiring the Scenery" has three
characters, a sanguine priest, a choleric "small man," and a melancholy
main character named Hanafan—in the background there is a phlegmatic station-porter to complete things. The three are teachers who
have walked into the countryside on a day off and are awaiting the
train back to Newtown. As they wait, Hanafan announces the
question for discussion: do ordinary people admire the scenery around
them, which leads him to the not-unrelated declaration that every
man lives out his own imagination of himself. The rest of the story is
an *exemplum*, told by Hanafan, concerning the behavior of a stage-

struck former stationmaster at this very station who fancied himself to have a fine voice and who one night kept singing from the platform to the people on an arriving train so ardently that he allowed the train to pass right through the station without stopping. Thus the stationmaster lived out his conception of himself as more than a stationmaster—as a spellbinding singer, he ignores the "scenery" and gives full throat to his inner spirit. And by extension, Hanafan implies, so should they all in a country where everything is always going wrong. He espouses subjectivism in preference to social interaction.

But there is a second and more hidden story layered beneath that of the stationmaster; it is the story of Hanafen himself for whom that same night was "so precious ... the he could not speak of it openly." For Hanafan was with a mysterious and since-lost "friend," no doubt a woman, to whom he recited, under the ravishing heavens, a passage from Sir Thomas Browne's *The Quincunx* which speaks of the sleeplessness of lovers. Apparently Hanafan missed his chance for permanent love on the same night that the stationmaster missed the train, and they both have ended up lonely men. *That* night was moon-drenched and quincunx-filled, not like the night of the primary story when rain is pouring "up the line" in Dublin. O'Faolain reflects here his own confusion and turmoil, his choice of personal over social reconciliation, the irony of one man's self-absorption being the cause of another man's distraction and of a stationmaster rather than his passengers missing the train, and, finally and most important, he laments the elusiveness of the ineffable muse and the bleakness of the future.

Fortunately, the confusion was to fall away in the half dozen years after *A Purse of Coppers* during which O'Faolain established his reputation once and for all and achieved power and importance as the editor of *The Bell*. He also decided what kind of writer he was going to be—his future output would include books on Ireland, which editors asked him for, and biography, autobiography, editing, and introduction-writing stints; these would keep the wolf from the door. But the main focus from here on would become the short story. The stories in his third and next volume of stories, *The Man Who Invented Sin* (1947), reflect a new clarity about human character, a new poignance of the sort that the short story among *genres* is particularly able to distill, and—at last—the special gold of Irish writing, humor.

O'Faolain's humor can be richly enjoyed in a story like "Teresa" where an immature, self-centered, and overly romantic young postulate is sent on a pilgrimage by the Mother Superior of her order to the shrine of St. Therese Martin at Lisieux for the purpose of testing the strength of her vocation.

Teresa is a pampered child who feels sorry for herself at every turn, yet who theatrically declares, "I want to be a saint!" Her models of sanctity are apparently from the cinema. When she stretches on the floor of her cell to meditate, her repose is noisily demolished by the discovery of an insect; when her traveling companion, old Sister Patrick, urges her to remain in the convent, she says that she can not, for "it is too worldly." But how is her order too worldly?, asks Sister Patrick. Because, says Teresa, "you all eat too much," stigmatizing in one instant the only lenity of Sister Patrick's life, eating sweets, and defecting in the next instant to have breakfast, in a tennis frock, with her sister-in-law in London.

But Teresa's best touch of blithe insincerity comes at the end, two years later, when she returns in material splendor for a visit to the convent with her Protestant husband. "You will never know what I gave up to marry you!" she assures George as he places a cigarette between her rouged lips. George can only slink off guiltily and explain to his colleagues at work in the morning that "his wife was 'a very spiritual woman' and on occasions like this she always made him feel that he had the soul of a boy." With "The Man Who Invented Sin," "Teresa" is a break-through into drolly rounded and satiric characterization for O'Faolain, the beginning of his most typical and successful work.

To take one other story from the same collection, one that shows O'Faolain's new facet of nostalgic wisdom, let us look for a moment at "Up the Bare Stairs." This is another "in the train" story, but in the mature manner of "Dividends" rather than in the diffused, gnomic manner of "A Broken World." That is to say, the ride from Dublin to Cork in this story, and in later ones, denotes a controlled moving back into the land of childhood, the realm of story: when O'Faolain takes us into the tunnel approaching Cork, what happens to him is equivalent to Alice's plunge down the rabbit hole. On the Cork train, he is mesmerized, profitably, by nostalgia, ready to penetrate his various encrustations and show his realest self. "If once the boy within us ceases to speak to the man who enfolds him," he writes in the closing lines of Vive Moi!, "the shape of life is broken and there is, literally, no more to be said."[15] To nostalgia O'Faolain here adds technical aplomb in using the time-honored device of the intriguing stranger met on the train who confides his deepest secrets. The personality of this character, the new baronet Francis James Nugent, comes across with seeming effortlessness—he is a spare, wintry, greying man whose bittersweet life has been lived out of spite. Humiliated years before in school by his mercurial teacher Brother Angelo, Nugent was thereafter chastised by his perfectionist parents, an experience that blighted for all time the possibility of his enjoying the fun and fancy of a normal boyhood. He has compensated for his single, traumatic youthful deficiency in Euclid by living out a mechanical life in pursuit of success, and he has replicated the whirring of his parents' sewing machines by making himself a robot.

The story is deeply moving, a heart-rending dissection of pity and spite when they are carried to their farthest extreme. In renouncing the narrowness and poverty of his parents—in moving outward in life from the dead geranium on the landing to their loft—Sir Francis has ironically choked off for life the flow of his own natural affection. He lives for imaginary retaliation against people who wished him only well. As he explains: "I hated my mother and I hated my father from the day that they made me cry. They did to me the one thing that I couldn't stand up against. They did what that little cur Angelo planned they'd do. They broke my spirit with pity." The parents silently sought their son's pity, used it to goad him upward in the world. Now Nugent returns to Cork from London with his mother's corpse, his heart still twisted with thwarted love. Back toward the womb of pain he goes as the train plunges into the tunnel, the amniotic water dripping from the air vents in the darkness, the narrator complimenting him on showing pity to his mother!

Nugent gets off the train at the end after donning a new silk topper and black scarf that he takes from a monogrammed leather hat box. He exits onto the platform to meet his mother's people, "a bent old woman . . . in a black shawl, and three or four humble-looking men in bowler hats and caps. As I watched him bow to them and doff his hat to the old woman and introduce himself, the yellow pine-and-brass of the coffin was already emerging from the van . . . " Monogrammed leather for himself, pine for his mother as she is ejected dumbly into the midst of her relatives in a painfully ironic reverse-birth ritual. Surely Nugent is wishing, too late, that his mother could see his triumphal return—he's done what she wanted him to; and surely O'Faolain demonstrates in this story a new profundity towards the heart's devious ways, one commensurate with that caught by Yeats in the poem ("The Pity of Love") from which O'Faolain takes the story's epigraph: "A pity beyond all telling is hid in the heart of love."

The irony and ambiguity of human emotions suffuse the stories of *The Man Who Invented Sin*; they tell of the streak of astringency inevitably at the center of the generous heart. "Unholy Living and Half Dying" and "The End of a Good Man" are good examples of this same thesis, as they are of O'Faolain's wit and intelligence. So is the quietly beautiful and mocking story "Passion"[16] in which the six lovely lillies that are the pride and joy of the narrator's uncle are battered into the mud by a rainstorm after the uncle denies the entreaties of neighborhood mourners who want the lillies for the wake of a dead child. Owning a thing means pain, means that it owns us, as Thoreau once said. Enlightenment ignored and wisdom gained too late become staples of O'Faolain's middle stories.

Likewise typical is "Lord and Master" from *The Finest Stories* (1957) which contains a half-dozen strong character portrayals, the chief one being the schoolmaster of the title. The retired master's autocratic manner is at first highly funny, reminiscent in fact of Lynn Doyle's bibulous pedagogue in Doyle's Ballygullion stories because, like him, Master Kennedy has taught all the townsmen and can still exert his old power of intimidation over them. Kennedy is arrogant in the way he demands that the town officials order the lake of Lord Carew drained since its overflow dampens the foundations of the gate cottage he rents. But O'Faolain soon shows himself to be out of sympathy with the master's claim of his "rights." Carew turns out to be selling his estate to an order of nuns; the lake will be drained and its bed put into cultivation; Carew *has* to sell the estate that his family has owned for two hundred and fifty years because he is going broke and dying. Generously, Carew grants Kennedy the hospitality of his manor when the latter grows suddenly ill, and then drives him around the lovely lake at nightfall on the way to the gate cottage. Kennedy has turned the town over for nothing: his habit of seeing the threat of Carew's power in everything from the solicitor's gesture with his hands—as if he were saying *Dominus vobiscum*—to the local monsignor's haughtiness is laughable and, ultimately, mean-minded.

One hears O'Faolain's parody of Simon Dedalus at the Christmas dinner-table in the master's rant to the monsignor: "... the Church is against us! As the Church was always against us. Against the Fenians. The men of forty-eight. Parnell. Sinn Fein. In the fight for the Republic ... " Unobstrusively the story turns serious. A silly old man's humbug is seen in contrast to a dying old man's wistful dignity.

Witness O'Faolain's stylistic quicksilver as the two old adversaries look out over the lake from Carew's drawingroom:

> Behind the haze of fishing flies on Carew's tweed hat [Kennedy] saw an oblong sheet of water burning below its low granite coping, fiery in the sun that was sinking between a rosy scallop of clouds and the flowing hills of Villy, now as hard as jewels in the cold April air. Its long smooth glow was broken only by a row of cypresses at its far end, the reflection of whose black plumes plunged into the burning pool to spear the light again. Beneath them there were two wrestling Tritons from whose mouths two fountains rose, and crossed and fell with a soft splash. Carew watched the old man's eyes for a moment or two. They were a play of astonishment, delight, and hate. "Well, Mr. Kennedy, there's the cause of it all. And you're looking at it for, I think, the first time? And, probably, for the last time."

The astonishment, delight, and hate felt by the master are only a part of the emotional melange that O'Faolain so faultlessly combines in this story, indeed one of his finest. And as in his earliest stories, we see here once more his bittersweet regret toward the diminishing fortunes of the Anglo-Irish gentry.

To turn to his next book of stories, desire is the emotion that O'Faolain associates chiefly with memory in the eleven short works of *I Remember! I Remember!* (1961).[17] The association is decidedly not Eliotic but, rather, reflects O'Faolain's contention—argued throughout the book—that bending one's memories for convenience's sake is salubrious and, in fact, essential. Otherwise, as happens to Sarah Cotter in the title story, what one remembers perfectly is "all untrue in the way that a police report is untrue, because it leaves out everything except the facts." Sarah is plagued, or rather plagues others, with total recall. O'Faolain's point is that anything perfect in mankind is monstrous. As he puts it in a sentence reminiscent of F. Scott Fitzgerald: "What keeps her [Mary] from visiting Sarah more often is the tireless whispering of the Recording Angel's Dictaphone playing back every lightest word that has passed between the two of them since they could begin to talk." In the end, Sarah's innocent perfection in eliciting details of her sister's sporadic indiscretions drives Mary to manufacture an excuse for cutting short her latest visit to Ardagh. Sarah intuits that it is the end of Mary's life-supporting visits from America—"I'll never see you again," she tells Mary. Mary draws the curtains across the dark windows with a dramatic swish and says icily: "You'll see me lots of times. Lots and lots of times." She won't be back—everyone knows it—and Sarah will go on seeing her in the relentless memory to which Mary now commits her.

In place of the Cork train tunnel, O'Faolain evokes the past in "I Remember! I Remember!" by picturing a cart passing slowly beneath the arch of the old North Gate while Mary watches and Sarah rehashes Mary's relationship with a married man: "The little cart emerged from under the arch, salmon-pink, bearing its pyramid of black peat, drawn by a tiny grey donkey. It *cric-crocked* slowly past her vision." It is a piquant figure: Mary's painful burden of memories being trotted out by the crippled Sarah with girlish asininity. Nice, too, is Mary's Proustian flashback as she recalls the wood ash that was blown into the cups of wine that Joe Fenelon stole from his father's shop on Midsummer Eve years before. Truly, O'Faolain has a deft feel for the fated randomness of such synapses of memory. We see it again when Sarah speaks to Mary of Mary's "poor friend, Mrs. Henry Beirne": "[Mary] knew no Mrs. Henry Beirne. Her frightened efforts to recall the woman produced nothing clearer than the vague cloud that a drop of absinthe forms in a glass of water, a fume like smoke, a wavering embryo without a face." Mary's "frightened efforts" lead her to a *dictum* that she once read in Stendhal's diaries: "True feeling leaves no memory," but this rationalization won't hold up in the face of Sarah's tenacity. Slowly the reader senses that Mary is in fact guilty of the various *innuendi* of Sarah's casual recollections. O'Faolain prompts us to ask, Who is ever innocent? Mary's sudden departure is much worse than any of her earlier mischiefs, for Sarah is left alone with her flawless instrument and nothing to exercise it upon—confined to a wheel-chair since she was eleven, she has no past of her own. Once again, O'Faolain agitates a deeper chord of pain and hopelessness in a story that starts as a droll comedy of domestic manners.

The same process of fated randomness and its bittersweet effects is O'Faolain's subject in the other superior story of *I Remember! I Remember!*, "A Touch of Autumn in the Air." The ambience of this story of hardly ten pages is clearly Chekhovian—we are reminded of O'Faolain's enthusiasm in *Short Stories: A Study in Pleasure* for "Gooseberries," for the way that Checkhov's hero seeks a life-long ideal until he achieves it, only to discover that he has himself altered in the course of the pursuit. Old Daniel Cashen, successful blanket manufacturer of Roscommon, exercises a selective memory as he talks to the narrator,

John, in the foyer of the town's hotel on a sunny day. Suddenly Dan is carried back in memory sixty years to the idyllic day that he sported among the ferns with his cousin Kitty. He and Kitty brought the mail—two letters from Kitty's brothers—out to Kitty's father and her third brother who were "ditching" a small meadow on the verge of the family property. While the letters go round, the two youngsters flirt and frolic. Kitty's brother Christopher, who is a seminarian in Dublin, writes that his old girl friend, Fanny Emphie, has entered the convent and become Sister Fidelia; she was unable to sleep well for the first few weeks, Christopher notes, presumably because of the new-to-her traffic noises of the city. Brother Owen is doing well as pit manager of the mine at Castlecomer. Kitty playfully makes a nun's cowl from a man's handerkerchief in imitation of Fanny as they gambol in the woods, but soon after she and Dan drive home in the donkey-cart, beneath the arched trees and "the honking of wild geeses called down from the north by the October moon." On the trek back, they stop for sweets which have the brand-name of "Conversation Lozenges," and it is this confection that triggers Dan's memory so many years later when he happens upon them in a candy-store.

A simple story of an old bachelor's chance memory in the autumn of life. Yet by a combination of vivid pictoralizing suggestions, O'Faolain leads the reader to suspect the extent of Daniel Cashen's sense of the deprivation of his whole adult life. For him the memory of Kitty and her relatives in the meadow is a spot of time, a moment when perfect human unity was apprehended: "It was a picture to be remembered for years: the meadow, the old man, the smoke of the distant farmhouse, patriarchal, sheltered, simple." All of life was there that day between morning and moonlight in the river bottom where "hundreds of streams and dykes" flowed together to form the basin of the river Barrow. Dan's own life, obviously, could itself have flowed along a different, better course. The paradigm of the men ditching in the primordial river, out of time, is lovingly and delicately developed by O'Faolain. One sees that Kitty's brothers—one gone to heaven, the other to hell, but both gone from the farm in what used to be called the "Queen's County"—represent poles of possibility for the young; that, when old Dan impulsively peers under the nun's cowl in the sweets-and-toys shop where his revery starts and comes upon the very old face of a total stranger, he is as young in desire as any fledgling courtier; and that the honking and wild geese are harbingers of winter and the passing of time, ultimately of the cold and beckoning grave.

For old Dan, despite his business success, life has gone down-
hill ever since, all the time that—like Tolstoy's Ivan Ilych—he thought
it was going upward. The overall effect of his revery is to confirm his
insight into the littleness of his life, and he dies one week later. It is a
masterfully dry yet full-bodied story, the *blanc de blanc* of the collection. The reader is left to muse over many understated images of time
and loss such as the light of the "lovely summer day" the crisp sway of
which is usurped by the distant moon, or the decelerating "revolving
glass doors" of the hotel that flash with "the whole movement of the
universe since time began," or the woolen blankets that Cashen had
made his refuge after the green ferns once covered him and Kitty, or
the veiny ditches and streams struggling to the open sea. The story is
sad, and lovely, and near perfect in its depth of feeling.

If memory is O'Faolain's touchstone in *I Remember! I Remember!*,
atmosphere is his prime concentration in the ten new stories of his next
collection, *The Heat of the Sun* (1966). The thick feel of surrounding
things—of texture, weather, comforting and discomforting environ-
ments—is the emphasis here. The two best stories of the collection
seem to me to be the title story and "Dividends." In the first, Johnny
Kendrick, a merchant sailor, returns to the warm wood and glass of his
favorite pub south of Dublin but finds that Alfie, the bartender who
had always in the past held his group of drinking cronies together, is
in the Hospice for the Dying with cancer. The group impetuously goes
around to offer comfort to the bartender's estranged wife, and, after
the departure of the others, Johnny falls asleep next to her in bed. But
Johnny's thoughts are all of the beautiful tease Deirdre, a sometime
member of the pub group who has deserted it in search of men who
can give her expensive love-tokens like sport cars; thus the jilted
Johnny and the bartender's widow-to-be are, to one another, substi-
tutes in time of need for the companions they really crave.

When Johnny awakens suddenly at 5 A.M., he finds Alfie's wife
sitting in Alfie's overcoat by the cold fire and damp window, instinctively sure that Alfie has died in the night. The heat of the sun—the
warmth of companionship and fellow-feeling—now denied to Alfie is
likewise extinguished from the midst of the drinking group *in toto* by
Alfie's death. As Johnny goes home through the damp night, his
prospects now dashed, he stops to view a blackened "coal-tub" in the
Coal Harbour—another reminder of his grimy nomad life—as a dawn
jet roars out of Dublin above him. Amid the warm interiors of the bar
scenes, the "gleam of the bottles and the wet mahogany, and the slow,

floating layers of smoke," O'Faolain gradually chips away at his protagonist's vagrant hopes, shows him forced to learn the transiency of affection, the fragility of expectation. The story has a roller-coaster structure down from the boozy insulation of the pub to the deathly Coal Harbour, where everything comes to dust. It is a story with a *frisson* of terror, of the sun burning off and Johnny finding that he, like us all, is becoming like Alfie.

A particularly amusing and "O'Faolainesque" story is "Dividends" which signals the author's achievement in the 1960's of his highest plateau of quality. The story has rather a small amount of plot in keeping with O'Faolain's asseveration in his first article on "The Craft of the Short Story"[18] that he regards plot as being low on the scale of technical embellishments. In brief, the narrator's aunt, a poor woman all her life, sells the stock she inherits but continues to call every month on her broker, Mel Meldrum, to collect the dividends on it. Sean comes to Cork at Mel's urgent request (through the inexorable tunnel) and stays the weekend at Mel's regal "cottage" on the outskirts of the city. But Sean can't make Aunt Anna see her illogic about the dividends—he can only enjoy Mel's argumentative hospitality while he observes Mel's compromising relationship with his housekeeper-typist, Sheila. The story, which is one of O'Faolain's longer ones, ends with Sean's departure for Dublin after Mel's statement of intention to "sack" Sheila and hire the redoubtable Anna as his housekeeper.

The *real* focus of the story is on the moral and ethical disputes between Mel and Sean, the two old schoolmates whom O'Faolain uses to spotlight the dipoles and angularities of Irish attitude and belief. O'Faolain's achievement in "Dividends" is in encompassing with ease so much dynamism during one sunny weekend in June when a whole people, including four individuals, are seen to stand at a crossroads. O'Faolain's best mature work seems full-blown and discursive in manner of presentation, yet actually it is tauter than his earlier stories. "Dividends" turns on a "crossroads" in as fortuitous and expert a manner as O'Connor, the master of the crossroads device, ever employed it; and yet the story goes beyond that toward Stendhal's conception of prose narrative as a "mirror being carried along a highway."

Chief among the contrasts that figure in the story is that between Mel, a "precise, piercing, priggish, and prim" Corkonian, who is a self-described realist, and the more worldly Sean from Dublin who is thought (wrongly) by Mel to be a dreamy romancer. Despite his wealth and Oxford education, Mel has a provincial and narrow-minded streak, and these are the liabilities that Sean has overcome since his move to the capital and his taking on the mantle of artist. (Just behind Sean lurks O'Faolain, mulling through the proxies of Sean and Mel the disparity between his actual life and the road-not-taken.)

Mel flaunts his substance, such as his ostentatious white Jaguar, but Ireland is not ready for such *chic*, as we see when his car is impeded in the middle of the city by a flock of bullocks and drovers, and as we see definitively when he tries to "reason" with dotty Aunt Anna from the country. His sumptuous house and style are too out of scale with Anna's slum flat and Sheila's laborer's cottage to go unnoticed by anyone except him. In fact, Mel's money changes both of their ways of life: Anna begins to change for the worse when she sees Mel's brokerage with its Turkish carpet—she uses her stock settlement to splurge foolishly on a fur coat. Sean finds her playing the role of "a Country Lady in reduced circumstances" and pretending that she was formerly a member of the gentry. So too Sheila is swept beyond her natural romantic restraints by Mel, who is twice her age; he comes between her and her motor-biking boy-friend. In short, Mel tends to humiliate people with his money; Sheila and Anna, who are seen by the narrator to be younger and older versions of one type of person, are made into Irish servants by it.

To sum up, the contrasts and character changes portrayed so subtly by O'Faolain come to rest in the corrosive effects of Mel's wealth which has made him unnoticing of human grief. Sean is brought in by O'Faolain to correct his understanding and prepares himself by contemplating his own values from the wall of a quay on the Lee before carrying them home to edify the errant Mel. At bottom, "Dividends" is a thinly cloaked assault by O'Faolain on modernism, egotism, vulgarity, and impersonality—it is a testimonial to a decent, reflective, unselfish viewpoint. What Sean must finally teach Mel is the right way to live. It is the logical outcome of their schoolboy philosophical discussions.

At Mel's cottage, Sean listens to the *Siegfried Idyll* as Mel comes in from taking Sheila home—it is the same music that later is to course through the house and awaken Sean at two A.M. The reader recalls O'Faolain's use of Mozart's *Don Giovanni* in "Midsummer Night Madness" to "awaken" another, younger Sean (then still called John). Here the music evokes both the lovely story of Wagner's devotion to his Cosima—a December-and-May match like that of Mel and Sheila—

and the sad romance of Brunhilde languishing in Valhalla until she is delivered by her lover's kiss.

Sean says of the music, " . . . it made me wish to God I was at home in bed with my wife. . . ." The replacement of Mozart's rake in the earlier story by the heroic Siegfried in this one suggests a mellowing in O'Faolain. Ultimately, Nestorian Sean manages to rekindle Mel's pity; he tells Mel to kick out on the rubbish heap "that fancy portrait of an unbreakable, incorruptible, crusty, self-absorbed old man, stiff-necked with principles and pride and priggishness." In the end, Mel's "most secret dream" of vanity and power over the two women and the world in general is uncovered and destroyed by Sean. Mel comes to believe his own advice to his clients: a real investor knows that he must take a risk on accumulating dividends rather than coldly insuring fixed profits. "Dividends" succeeds because of its amusing interplay of characters, its atmosphere of fellowship-amid-plenty in Mel's suburban "cottage" and pity-amid-squalor in Aunt Anna's Cork slum, and because it disguises its moralizing beneath blankets of humorous and sophisticated prose.

O'Faolain was to re-emphasize gentle preachment and worldly style in his seventh volume of stories, *The Talking Trees* (1970). Of the three best stories in the collection—"Hymeneal," "The Time of Their Lives," and "Of Sanctity and Whiskey"—the two last mentioned are unmistakably in O'Faolain's late vein. "The Time of Their Lives" concerns a pair of over-the-hill lovers in Italy, both from formerly wealthy families, who break up after a brief, touching romance; "Of Sanctity and Whiskey" is a sardonic farce about a besotted Irish painter who returns to his old college to paint the portrait of his former teacher and drinks himself to death in the process of doing so.

Almost as sardonic is "Hymeneal" which is one of O'Faolain's most powerful domestic dramas. The point of the story doesn't emerge until the end when Phil Doyle is asked to sort out the effects of his boss, brother-in-law, and supposed best friend, Failey Quigley, who has been killed in a car crash. Phil returns reluctantly to Dublin from rural Clare where he has just moved with his wife Abby and spends the whole night after the funeral pouring over Failey's intimate papers in a scene protracted by O'Faolain. Phil, we learn, bristled throughout his career as Inspector of Primary Schools at the stupidity of all his superiors, including Failey, but his contempt for the dead man whom he had always thought of as an "ingratiating, devious, ambitious, convivial" opportunist slowly evaporates as Phil comes to realize that Failey was really his long-time secret benefactor.

Phil's discovery makes him grow more and more agitated; it is pure gall for him to have to feel admiration and gratitude toward any man, especially the successful Failey. Plunging into the rainy street, he re-visits his old house on the North Circular Road, the house which—Phil discovers from going through Failey's effects—Failey bought back again for him and for Abby with whom Failey once had a love affair. Phil returns to Failey's study chastened by the cleansing rains. He dons Failey's old dressing-gown and overcoat while his own clothes dry and descends in the morning to the kitchen to sit in Failey's breakfast place where he is doted upon by Abby and Failey's widow. The marriage song of O'Faolain's wistful title will be sounded over Phil and Abby's second-honeymoon in their old house, one feels, and their new union blessed by the softening of Phil's crabby and envious nature.

"Hymneal" is a great-hearted story, though never cloying; its point is that wisdom may come belatedly as a compensation for other losses, that kindness needn't be beyond our expectations—and that with age comes a richness not known earlier in life. And O'Faolain practices what he preaches: Phil Doyle had planned for years to write as his pet project during retirement "The Book," a poisonous autobiographical expose that would settle all of his old accounts with the fools he had suffered for a lifetime. Now Phil won't write "The Book," and neither will O'Faolain, as he moves into old age, surrender his bittersweet but cheerful and compassionate outlook on life.

The same amused and humane outlook is maintained throughout the stories of O'Faolain's most recent collection, *Foreign Affairs* (1975), published in his seventy-fifth year. As in *The Talking Trees*, the characteristic note is sardonicism (the word comes from a Sardinian plant said to produce laughter so compulsive that death results, a plant whose cousin is named woody nightshade or—the key descriptive epithet for O'Faolain—bittersweet). Constantly we find pleasure mixed with regret, laughter with pain, never with rancor or animosity. O'Faolain's late stories are soft-hearted but never soft-headed, still rooted in the comedy of manners, more crisply cosmopolitan, more frank and sadly accepting and worldly than his earlier.

Here, for instance, is the opening paragraph of the first story of *Foreign Affairs*, "The Faithless Wife":

> He had now been stalking his beautiful Mlle. Morphy,
> whose real name was Mrs. Meehawl O'Sullivan, for six

weeks, and she had appeared to be so amused at every stage of the hunt, so responsive, *entrainante*, even *aquichante*, that he could already see the kill over the next horizon. At their first encounter, during the St. Patrick's Day cocktail party at the Dutch embassy, accompanied by a husband who had not a word to throw to a cat about anything except the scissors and shears that he manufactured somewhere in the West of Ireland, and who was obviously quite ill at ease and drank too much Irish whiskey, what had attracted him to her was not only her splendid Boucher figure (whence his sudden nickname for her, La Morphée), or her copper-colored hair, her lime-green Irish eyes and her seemingly poreless skin, but her calm, total and subdued elegance: the Balenciaga costume, the peacock-skin gloves, the gleaming crocodile handbag, a glimpse of tiny, lace-edged lawn handkerchief and her dry, delicate scent. He had a grateful eye and nose for such things. It was, after all, part of his job.

The "He" of the first word is the French diplomat Ferdinand Clichy, a histrionic lover whose headlong affair with Celia O'Sullivan comes to an end when her husband has a permanently debilitating stroke and she, out of pity, refuses to desert him. Never was O'Faolain's hand for character-drawing surer as when the romance of the adulterous middle-aged lovers picks up momentum. Having reached the supposed candor of mature years, Celia and Ferdy actually prefer the delicious guilt of make-belief. "Your trick is to be innocence masquerading as villainy," Ferdy says to her, insisting that she use signals such as "Three red geraniums in a row on the windowsill" to let him know that the coast is clear: "He could, she knew, have more easily checked with her by telephone, but . . . she accepted with an indulgent amusement what he obviously considered ingenious devices for increasing the voltage of passion by the trappings of conspiracy."

The whole story, as O'Faolain structures it, is a tease, the movement of which is kept slow but pointed to the end where the impossibility of Celia and Ferdy's affair becomes manifest to them. Then the author closes down the narrative perfunctorily. O'Faolain is instinctively not a writer to attenuate the painful implications of the lovers' split-up nor to reach out for coy and sentimental finales after the comedy ends. Rather, the break-up is prompted by Celia who answers Ferdy's final epistolary attestation that "You are the love of my life!" with the fatalistic Irishism, "Don't *I* know it?"

To sum up, O'Faolain's favorite subject is the mating of late-

October with late-October, of Anthonys and Cleopatras in well-cut
Irish tweeds. The co-ordinates of his prose are adjusted to the time
when commonsense flourishes but is troubled by passion, passion
that understands mutability. Then the wary are flushed out. O'Faolain's
ultimately homespun soul always softens the incrustations that the
world of sophistication tries to impose on his characters. The manifest
touchstones at the end of his writing career are a sardonic sense of life's
running comedy, especially in its mating institutions, a tender feeling
for the good things in life, and a penchant for late love. He gains in
heart and mind from beginning to end.

Notes

[1] Maurice Harmon, *Sean O'Faolain, A Critical Introduction* (South Bend:
University of Notre Dame, 1967) and Katherine Hanly, "The Short Stories of Sean
O'Faolain: Theory and Practice," *Éire*, 6:3 (Fall, 1971) 3-11.

[2] Joseph Storey Rippier, in *The Short Stories of Sean O'Faolain, A Study in
Descriptive Technique* (Garrands Cross, Bucks.: Colin Smythe, 1976), pp. 45-48, lists
a number of resemblances in style and manner between Joyce and O'Faolain.

[3] O'Faolain makes this distinction himself in the Foreward to *The Finest
Stories of Sean O'Faolain* (Boston: Little, Brown and Company, 1957), p.x. His view
is analogous to that of Frank O'Connor who called Ireland "Europe's sleeping-
beauty sister."

[4] O'Faolain, *Vive Moi!* (Boston: Little, Brown, and Company, 1964) 334.

[5] John Chamberlain, "Sean O'Faolain's Fine Tales of the Irish Rebellion," *The
New York Times* (March 27, 1932), 7.

[6] Harmon p. 156.

[7] O'Faolain expressed his international manifesto in *Studies*, LI (Spring,
1962) 102-103: "The lesson of our time is that Irish writers can no longer go on writing
about Ireland, or for Ireland, within the narrow confines of the traditional Irish life-
concept; it is too slack, too cozy, too evasive, too untense. They must, or perish as
regionalists, take, as writers everywhere do, the local (since they know its details
most intimately) and universalize it. . . ."

[8] O'Faolain, *Vive Moi!* p. 369.

[9] John V. Kelleher, "Sean O'Faolain," *The Atlantic* , vol. 199 (May, 1957), 69.

[10] O'Faolain, *The Finest Stories of Sean O'Faolain*, p. x.

[11] O'Faolain himself regards his characters ambivalently. In a letter to me
(August 15, 1979), he writes: "Alas, if I don't love my people I always pity them."
Then, written in by hand, "Damn them!"

[12] Valleys appear in several O'Faolain stories and, as in Ireland, often have lakes and islands in the midst of them. In O'Faolain's iconography, an island in a lake suggests Tir-n'an-Og (cf., *e.g.* "The Man Who Invented Sin," "The Silence of the Valley, and "Lovers of the Lake).

[13] See O'Faolain, "The Craft of the Short Story—3," *The Bell*, 7:6 (March, 1944), 534-35.

[14] Garnett, in his Introduction to *Midsummer Night Madness*, voices the criticism against Irish philistinism that has been commonplace among literary exiles from George to Brian Moore.

[15] O'Faolain, *Vive Moi!*, 374.

[16] O'Faolain apparently had second thoughts about this story—he chose it for inclusion in his second retrospective, *Selected Stories of Sean O'Faolain* (London: Constable, 1978), after omitting it from the first, *The Finest Stories of Sean O'Faolain* (1957). Somewhat inexplicably he also placed it among ten previously uncollected stories in *The Heat of the Sun* (1966) eighteen years after its original publication.

[17] There are at least two poems of the same name in anthologies but without exclamation points, one by Thomas Hood (1798-1845), the other by Winthrop Mackworth Praed (1802-1839). The former wrote: "I remember, I remember / How may childhood fleeted by, / The mirth of its December, / The warmth of its July."

[18] O'Faolain, "The Craft of the Short Story," *The Bell*, 7:4 (January, 1944), 337 *et seq.*

Chapter Four

The Sage Who Deep in Central Nature Delves:
Liam O'Flaherty's Short Stories

As a story writer, Liam O'Flaherty comes after Sean O'Faolain and Frank O'Connor in order of artistic worth, but he well preceded them as an established figure in the field. Four years older than O'Faolain and seven than O'Connor, O'Flaherty loosed a flood of prose work in the 1920's: he composed the main share of his fifteen novels and of his approximately 160 short stories in just one decade. His prodigious energy level flowed out of his return, in 1921, to the elemental life of Inishmore on Aran following years of wandering after World War I, and also out of his conviction in the early 1920s that he was destined to speak for his people:

> It seemed as if the dam had burst somewhere in my soul;
> for the words poured forth in a torrent. They came joy-
> ously and I felt exalted by their utterance, just as I used to
> feel when telling my mother some fantastic tale in my
> infancy.[1]

In the novel, his best work would not come until after the 1920s, beginning with *Skerrett* (1932); but in shorter fiction, the 73 stories in *Spring Sowing* (1924), *The Tent* (1925), and *The Mountain Tavern* (1929) stand out as O'Flaherty's best work in the form, along with the twenty new stories collected under the title *Two Lovely Beasts* in 1948.[2]

These four volumes considered together at once figure among the most and least "Irish" of the notable work produced in the Irish short story between its originators, Moore and Joyce, and its major living practitioners, O'Faolain and Lavin. They are among the most "Irish" stories because of their remarkably specific rendering of the folkways and social customs of Ireland's peasant population, the country's dominating population until the end of World War II. And yet, in several dozen cases these stories lack any suggestion whatever of place, time, or social environment. O'Flaherty's "Irish" stories have a native purity, an authority in dealing with the feel and smell and essence of peasant life that O'Faolain and O'Connor, for all their insight, cannot match. At the same time, many of his tales of birds and animals resemble notes from some eternal beast-book of prehensile creation, outside time, beyond the temporary egotisms of place.

At their most obvious, O'Flaherty's nature stories are celebrations of the workings of instinct and appetite, of the biological chain, and of the struggle of natural selection which often brings random death to living creatures but never dishonor. The only "bad" death comes from any effort to sidestep the power of nature. Of birds and fish, and animals and human beings, only the latter strive to thwart natural process because only they aspire to exploit other creatures in order to amass wealth. O'Flaherty's biological and genetic conservatism followed from his espousal of Marxist dialecticism in the 1920's. In their simplest form, his stories uphold the ethical merit of things as they are and authenticate D. H. Lawrence's vision of natural impulses as the Holy Ghost speaking in us and to us. Thus, the two-and-a-half-page story, "The Foolish Butterfly," might be regarded as a typical O'Flaherty nature story: the little butterfly, exulting in its young vigor and riding the wind as hungrily as Icarus, is blown out to sea. "Rejoicing once more in the wind and the heat and the light of the sun, it forgot its terror." When its strength wanes, the frail creature falls into the water and drowns. There is no implied regret in O'Flaherty's description of the way nature works; the story ends non-committally: "There were a few little movements of the round head. Then the butterfly lay still." But there is more to the story than an affirmation of nature, for in "The Foolish Butterfly," as in the preponderance of his nature and peasant stories, O'Flaherty dowers his creature with the Promethean attributes that constantly shine through in his work—courage and rebelliousness. Even as it falters, the butterfly is determined to strive, to seek, to find, and not to yield:

> Again it skimmed the surface of the sea with the curved ends of its trunk. Again it rose. It performed a frenzied series of little jumps, tossing itself restlessly on the heated air, exhausting the last reserves of its strength in a mad flutter of its beautiful white wings. Then it sank slowly despite fierce flopping. The wings dropped, swaying as they had done at the moment of birth when they had come from the chrysalis. The trunk touched the crest of the sea. It sank into the water. The wings fluttered once and then the sea-water filtered through them, like ink through blotting-paper.

What aggrandizes the seemingly insignificant butterfly is its resistance and struggle within the overwhelming hugeness of a benign but indifferent nature.   The quality admired throughout O'Flaherty's work is energy—the opposite of giving in to life. The highest good is to act, to take a chance, to "follow one's nature," as the saying goes. This viewpoint can be seen in the early story, "The Tramp," in which two paupers in a workhouse, educated "townies," are derided as burnt-out cases by a passing tramp, who ignores his own sordid past and blunders back into the world, trusting to his luck. The tramp knows that any kind of dependency is miserable. Likewise, in "The Landing," the three fishermen in the curragh strive to beach their boat in a storm. To Stephen Halloran's wife on the shore, they should never have gone out, for on this day twenty years before her grandfather died of pneumonia. Her superstition, like all superstition in O'Flaherty's work, makes men faint-hearted. The rowers, instead, beat into the heavy seas: "For a moment their cries surmounted the sound of the wind and the sea. It was the defiance of humanity hurled in the face of merciless nature." O'Flaherty shares Dostoievski's and Conrad's conviction that living is acting.[3]

Although man may attain the heights through action, O'Flaherty's early stories maintain a preference for the world of nature over the world of culture; only gradually does his compassion for the foibles of humanity come to rival his regard for nonhuman life. The well-known early story, "The Wren's Nest," is typical. The two boys, human marauders, smash the lovely nest and go on to other mindless destruction: "The inside [of the nest] was coated wonderfully with feathers and down, interlaced with an art that could not be rivalled by human beings. The boys tore it into shreds and scattered the shreds." More beautiful even than the wren's nest is the black mare in the story of that title. As Dan of the Fury describes her, "Her tail swept to the ground, and when the sun shone on her sides you could see them shimmering like the jewels on a priest's vestments; may the good God forgive me, a sinner, for the comparison. But what is nearer to God than a beautiful horse?" Certainly not a human being.

O'Flaherty's stories are studded with this same preference for the natural over the human. The title of "Sport: The Kill" bitterly reflects man's rationalization of taking life under the name of "sport." In the story, the helpless rabbit is flushed out to his death by the blood-thirsty boy, who does not need the meat to live, and by his dog, whose better nature has been turned against itself. In "Two Dogs," the thoroughbred greyhound is the less worthy competitor in a contest to catch a rabbit; the mongrel triumphs, and the greyhound dies, because the mongrel has not had his nature bred out by human show-dog refinement. Some boys trap a seagull with a baited line in "The Hook," but not for long: the gull's mate rightly bites the line in two and the story ends happily. When the revolting title character in "The Wild Sow" gorges herself illicitly on Neddy the Kilmillick fisherman's provisions, the reader recognizes that poetic justice has been done, for Neddy should have sold the pig when she was fat and young, rather than starving her until she bursts into his storeroom. Over and over, O'Flaherty reworks this theme of the superiority of instinctual bird and beast to human meanness and calculation in what might be called his "S.P.C.A. stories." Only nature is instructive: from the fecundity of the soil and the dumb beasts, man gains sustenance and the softening of his greed and blood-lust. This is the theme of O'Flaherty's first, great story, "Spring Sowing," in which the new wife broadcasts seed over the fertile ridges cut by her rutting husband, and of "Milking Time" in which, as in "Spring Sowing," the world of nature initiates the new couple "into the mysterious glamour of mating." Nature instantly purifies herself, as we see in O'Flaherty's treatment of mercy-killing in "The Wounded Cormorant," and usually instructs its human onlookers in the lessons of love, as in "Three Lambs" and "Birth."

These stories are not epistles to the animals and fishes. Surely they are intended to chasten and subdue, by holding up to scorn, the less agreeable tendencies of those who read them. Despite his very evident disdain for formal education, for priestcraft, for politicians and businessmen—in short, for the signs and figureheads of "civilization"—O'Flaherty finally proves himself to be neither moral nor misanthropic. He tries, rather, to shame the devil[4] in mankind and to hold up nature as a teacher and guide that will recall human behavior for the excesses of intellectualization. "Trapped," one of the best stories in the early volume *The Tent* (1926), aptly illustrates this attitude. Bartly Hernon escapes from the mountain fissure in which he is trapped by becoming first like a goat—"He had done a mighty thing. He had descended where no man ever had descended."—and then like a fish as he makes his way through a shark-infested part of the ocean—"He began to swim with all his strength, swimming on his side, heaving through the water with a rushing sound like a swan." Conversion to animalness produces his salvation, but human vanity reasserts itself in the last sentence of the story as the saved Bartly offers thanksgiving: "...while he prayed he kept thinking of what the village people would say of his heroic feat."

Human motives are most often mendacious in O'Flaherty's stories. When, in "The Hawk," the predatory bird catches a lark and takes it back to his nursing mate, we have a sense of nature fulfilled, but when the predatory egg-gatherer kills the hawk and makes off with his mate and her eggs, our anger rises at man's imbecile ruthlessness. The hawk acted against its own kind out of natural appetite and necessity, the man out of needless cruelty in the name of "sport." The poignancy of the story derives from our viewing it from the hawk's viewpoint. Nature, in tracing out its huge diurnal course, constantly gives man back good for bad. This is the theme of "The Tide" which simply describes the ocean's ecological reclamation of a beach after it is befouled by every sort of human litter. Perhaps O'Flaherty's most mystical story on nature as human benefactor is to be found in "The Mirror," which first appeared in 1953. Here a young girl becomes accidentally wet and strips to dry her clothes. Seeing herself naked for the first time in a mountain pool, she sensually awakens to an anticipation of her biological mission in a florid passage that evokes the worst of Lawrence:

> Aie! Aie! Miraculous chalice of life! Now she brooded in proud delight over the beauty she had seen in the strangeness of the deep dark water. She felt pleased in her heart's deepest core at the loveliness that had been bestowed on her, in order that she might be able to fulfill the mystery of her womb.
>
> Aie! Aie! A radiant virgin wantoning naked in the sunlight on silken moss and no longer afraid in the least of love's awe-inspiring fruit, the labour of pregnancy.

It is as if the myth of sea-born Venus Aphrodite had been taken up by some social-realist choreographer for a revolutionary ballet, right down to the bird screams. Yet, O'Flaherty's point is clear: the beauty of the world is in nature; human beauty finds its true correspondence and biological model there.

O'Flaherty's distinctive strengths and weaknesses are clear enough. Among the former we may list his skill at distilling stories to their essences, his ability to convey the important emotions affectingly, and his power of identifying the hidden communion between human beings and other living creatures. Among his shortcomings number imprecisions of eye and ear, a tendency to oversimplify plots, a persistent exaggeration of the line between human and animal behavior, and a habit of directing at adult audiences some stories better fitted for juvenile readers.

The strengths are hardly insignificant achievements. O'Flaherty's gifts of restraint and economy in storytelling often defy comparison among short story writers right back to his chief progenitor, Maupassant. His stories practically all focus either on life, on death, or on rebirth. His subjects are eternal and elemental; *vide* stories such as "His First Flight," about a fledgling gull pushed by its mother from its perch and forced to try its wings, or "The Cow's Death" in which a cow throws itself off a cliff into the sea in the vain hope of protecting its dead calf, which is about to be dragged off the rocks below by the tide, or "The Hook," "The Wild Goat's Kid," "The Mouse," and "The Grey Seagull," in all of which grave threats are avoided at a dire moment and life is allowed to resume. These are all stories of only a couple of pages, not so much anecdotes as vignettes of action charged with danger. Not only does O'Flaherty concentrate on the extreme moments of life and death, but he also writes largely about the extreme age groups, old people and children, flung off to the antipode of Europe and gripped by basic and extreme impulses such as hunger, hatred, greed, and sexual passion. His cameo art is the farthest thing from the warm social expansiveness of O'Connor and O'Faolain, as two stories of the 1940s demonstrate: "Life," in which a child is born while the grandfather of the family is dying, and "Light," in which the sun comes up and birds and animals stir, while a naked couple run from their tent, swim, and copulate beneath the blazing sun.

The price paid for O'Flaherty's less-is-more art lies mainly in character development, which is sometimes disastrously foreshortened, but, then, his characters are usually emanations of Everyman, and Everyman cannot bear much individuation. Rather than character, O'Flaherty's forte is action and the emotion that produces an action and is in turn colored by it. Hemingway is famous for his precise ordering of action and emotion; O'Flaherty, who admired him, is as good at it. In this excerpt from a very early story, "The Rockfish," the hunger, curiosity, courage, and sense of danger of the fish are suggested, along with the suppressed anticipation and excitement of the fisherman:

> A little rockfish came rushing out from a cavern under
> the rock. He whisked his tail and stopped dead behind a
> huge blade of seaweed when he saw the glistening baits.

> His scaly red body was the colour of the weed. It tapered
> from the middle to the narrow tail and to the triangular-
> shaped head. He stared at the baits for a long time without
> moving his body. His gills rose and fell steadily. Then he
> flapped his tail and glided to the upper hook. He touched
> it with his snout. He nibbled at it timorously three times.
> Then he snatched at the top of it and darted away back into
> the cavern with a piece of periwinkle in his mouth. The
> man on the rock sat up excitedly, threw his pipe on the rock,
> and seized the rod with both hands, breathing through his
> nose.

The poised moment of silent communion between the hungry and
wary fish below and the excited and waiting man above gives the
scene its suspense and truth. This same kind of communion became
O'Flaherty's stock-in-trade. Very few writers can match his power to
transmit the way the simultaneous strangeness and familiarity of
animals frighten and delight humans. A passage of vintage O'Flaherty,
from "Three Lambs," presents a ewe giving birth to a lamb, thereby
causing rapture in a watching boy who is not above remembering the
prize of three pancakes posted by his father for the first one to see the
new lamb:

> Little Michael sighed with delight and began to rub its
> body with his fingernails furiously. The sheep turned
> around and smelled it, making a funny happy noise in its
> throat. The lamb, its white body covered with yellow
> slime, began to move, and presently it tried to stand up, but
> it fell again and Little Michael kept rubbing it, sticking his
> fingers into its ears and nostrils to clear them. He was so
> intent on his work that he did not notice the sheep had
> moved away again, and it was only when the lamb was
> able to stand up and he wanted to give it suck, that he
> noticed the sheep was lying again, giving birth to another
> lamb. 'Oh, you devil,' gasped Little Michael, 'six pancakes.'

Occasionally O'Flaherty goes too far: his animals become too
human or his humans too animal-like to be altogether credible. Thus,
the title character of "The Blackbird" comes to "the sudden realization
that he was making a fool of himself singing out there in complete
darkness when all the other birds were gone to bed"—a becoming but
unlikely self-awareness. The same sort of anthropomorphic breach
occurs in "The Jealous Hens"—"The six little hens went off their food
completely and spent the whole evening planning some thing or
other, with their heads close together, standing on one leg"—and "The

Black Bird's Mate"—"But the hen bird on the eggs still sat with the same look of drowsy happiness in her half-closed eyes"—as well as elsewhere. Concomitantly, "Wolf Lanigan's Death"—an ancestor of *The Informer*, which O'Flaherty published a year later in 1925—features a title character so unbelievably savage—no doubt based on Jack London's Wolf Larson—that one wonders why no one has killed him before.

That O'Flaherty should succumb occasionally to such extremeness is understandable when he is working so close to the horns of the bull, so to speak. Far more damaging can be problems with plotting, specifically O'Flaherty's habit of imposing an oversimplified, chockablock plot upon some of his stories before forcing home a melodramatic conclusion, and of making his plots so cryptic and thin as to be ineffable. The first tendency is exemplified by a story like "The Sniper," identified by A. A. Kelly as O'Flaherty's first story to arouse public notice.[5] In this tale, a Republican marksman atop a building near O'Connell Bridge during the Civil War callously picks off three people, the third of whom turns out unsurprisingly to be the sniper's own Free Stater brother. In a related story, "Civil War," the irony is again troweled on: Jim Dolan stays a fellow soldier, a bully whom he hates, from the cowardly act of firing down from a rooftop at a number of unsuspecting enemy soldiers below. The bully is then himself shot three times from below and the enemy soldiers ascend to the roof to ungratefully kill their unknown protector, Dolan. Many stories suffer from severe plot anemia, such as "Poor People," "The Alien Skull," "The Sinner," "The Little White Dog," and "The Letter." To sample just one, in "The Letter," a poor family's daughter who has gone to America sends home twenty pounds, money that has, however, been earned by prostitution. At the end, the father of the family reads her tear-soaked letter: "His back was towards them but they knew he was crying. He had stood that way, apart, the year before, on the day their horse died." Stories like these seem juvenile and jejune, but then the stories of many writers composed in the heyday of literary naturalism now strike us as strained and mechanical. Mainly, O'Flaherty's stories of the period of the Troubles are over-adorned with dated naturalistic *impedimenta*. There are only about half a dozen of these. They always lack the sort of easy grace and worldliness that O'Faolain and O'Connor demonstrate in their early stories of the Troubles—"Guests of the Nation" and "Midsummer Night Madness." On the other hand, other stories of O'Flaherty's that stand outside the naturalist inclination compare

quite favorably with those written in the manner of which O'Faolain
and O'Connor were acknowledged masters. "The Eviction," for instance, has the same bittersweet wryness, while dealing with the same
subject matter, as "Midsummer Night Madness." "The Old Woman,"
about a buoyant old woman who carries her burial shroud about her
neck, approaches O'Connor's "The Long Road to Ummera" in express-
ing nobility of spirit. Read end-to-end, O'Flaherty stories offer fre-
quent flourishes of adaptability and range which his singleminded-
ness in pursuing an overall theme of survival would seem to limit.

One delightful example of O'Flaherty's adaptability may be
found in his humor, which occurs mainly in his stories about the
conniving of country people to win some small test over those just
above them in the social order and, so, to win a victory over the harsh
conditions of their life. Such a formulation is identical, of course, with
the way that much of the humor in Irish literature—or any literature
that deals with a submerged population striking back in covert
political retaliation at a master class—works. If art is a weapon, as
Lenin said, humorous art is the perfect weapon, because it defies
reprisal—the upper-caste victim must accept his lot or lose face.
O'Flaherty's humor sometimes is gentle and redemptive. In "The Old
Hunter," an eccentric horse, purchased for thirty shillings and un-
loaded on an unsuspecting rich man for thirty pounds, in fact helps the
rich man recover his health. A much more acrimonious type of folk
humor typifies the tale of Michael Feeney, called "Stoney Batter" by his
fellow villagers in the story of that title. Stoney strikes back at his
brother Peter, the gombeen man of the village, after Peter connives
successfully to get his miserable cottage, his only possession, away
from him. But the easygoing Stoney talks his housekeeper into
naming Peter as the father of her child, and it is Peter that the parish
priest makes "pay the bastardy." Peter has one arrow left: he evicts
Stoney from the cottage, but this is still another miscalculation by
Peter, for the town turns its contempt on him for hard-heartedness to
his brother. The gombeen man has violated the ancient order of the
village by acquiring property that was his brother's by right of
primogeniture. Peter lives on under a cloud of contumely, known to
the villagers as "the old ram," while he lets the victimized Stoney
expire in the workhouse. They both endure a perverse, mocking fate.

O'Flaherty's humorous narratives hardly ever prove as serpen-
tine as "Stoney Batter." In "The Bath," Paddy-the-Boots connives to
cadge a large number of drinks from the vinous barrister Campbell,

who has awakened to find himself unaccountably in a hotel a hundred miles from Dublin where he had begun drinking the day before. All the gentleman wants is a bath, but Paddy sees to it that his only liquid will be alcohol. The interplay between master and servant and their regularly reversing attitudes of intimidation and servility are triumphs of humorous art. No doubt O'Flaherty's comedy is better when he plays it quite broad. In "The Post Office," three sophisticated travellers enter a tiny country post office in Connemara and demand to send a telegram, in Spanish, to Los Angeles. Many of the people of the town happen to be assembled in the post office, for it is pension day, and they delight in observing the patent exasperation of the postmaster, Martin Conlon, who is devastated by any request at any time to send a telegram: "They would rather listen to him than to a fiddler while he was engaged in that work." Various strident characters of the town have amusing walk-on parts while Conlon fumes, and one of the travellers ends up transmitting the message in his stead. This story first appeared in *The Bell* in 1954; all of the townspeople bask in O'Flaherty's affectionate regard, especially his comic butt, Conlon, and the story well reflects its author's mellowing in the second half of his writing career. As happens with many writers, humor came to O'Flaherty with age.

While humor constitutes one of O'Flaherty's special gifts, it is a sidelight to his main line of endeavor, which is to display men and beasts maintaining their independent natures in the face of collective pressures to regiment them. The outsider practicing his individualism courageously and at whatever cost is his constant subject, as courage is his chief theme. Although this subject and theme become predictable in O'Flaherty's stories, they do not fall into triteness. Almost any cross-section of his stories offers evidence of these elements, from "The Reaping Race" of 1924, in which Michael Gill ignores ridicule from all sides to win a tortoise-and-hare contest in his own way, to "The Test of Courage" and "Two Lovely Beasts" of the 1940s. In the first of these latter two, a boy finds himself in a curragh helplessly drifting away from the Irish coast, tired, thirsty, and very possibly beyond the chance of rescue:

> Yet he experienced an exaltation that made him impervious to this torture. Ever since his imagination had begun to develop, he had been plagued by the fear that he would not be able to meet danger with courage. . . . Now the big test had come, [and] he experienced the first dark rapture of manhood instead of fear.

In "Two Lovely Beasts," Colm Derrane starves himself and his family
in order to rise in the world; in doing so, he ignores the town's obloquy.
However, Derrane's gradual rise is admirable not because of its
material accomplishment but, rather, as an acting out of man's isolated
and lofty determination. The townsmen turn their back on Derrane
for a second time, at the end, when his prosperity again increases.
Derrane disregards their taunts and simply moves away from them,
as he has been doing in another sense for years:

> As Colm drove away in his new green jaunting car, quite a
> number of people whistled after him in hostility and deri-
> sion. . . . His gaunt blue eyes looked completely unaware
> of their jeers. His pale blue eyes stared fixedly straight
> ahead, cold and resolute and ruthless.

O'Flaherty reiterates the same theme of indominance in animal
stories like "Prey," "The Fairy Goose," and "The Black Rabbit." In "The
Stone," only the hero "alone of all these strong men raised [the stone]
to his throat and kissed it with his lips three times," an action that
marks him off for the rest of the villagers from the rest of his life and
assures him of his own specialness. In "The Child of God" and "The
Flute Player," a painter and a musician willingly give up everything
for their artistic ideals. Throughout his work, the code of self-testing
and obstinate courage is as omnipresent in O'Flaherty as in Hemingway.

Probably O'Flaherty's major benefaction to the Irish short story
is the plentitude of closely considered social detail that one finds in his
work, details of western and island life that complement in fiction the
documentary accounts of Maurice O'Sullivan and Peig Sayers, or the
sociological studies of Arensberg and Kimball. Who has portrayed the
ritual of emigration more authentically than O'Flaherty has done in
two stories written twenty-two years apart, "Going Into Exile" and
"The Parting"? Each facet of the first story comes into view with the
inevitability of a pathetic ceremony: the father's need to sponsor a last-
night social no matter how meager; the group of Mary Feeney's friends
sitting with her on her bed in an "uncomfortable position just to show
how much they liked her"; the father sprinkling the departing children
with holy water; Michael taking a piece of loose whitewash from the
wall and putting it in his pocket. "The Parting" tells of Michael Joyce's
separation from his impoversihed family in order to study for the
priesthood. His brother Martin will inherit their father's farm when he

marries the following spring, while Michael is fated to help "rear and educate the children Martin would beget." The poignancy of O'Flaherty's own boyhood separation from his poor family surely finds voice in the story's ending where Michael's "bitterness [is] terrible because his young heart knew that dark vows would make his parting final, forever and forever."

O'Flaherty catches the ethical values of island life emphatically in "The Black Mare." Here we are shown the special privileges of the priest and the sense of resentment that these cause, the feelings of inferiority of the proud island men in relation to people on the mainland, the special importance of horsemanship in making marriages and fortunes. O'Flaherty outlines death customs in "Offerings" in which "Life does not end with ... death. ... There are others who live on and they have customs and a common code of conduct that must be observed." In "Stoney Batter," the plot devolves on Stoney's need to see that his house gets "a thorough cleansing and renovating," for "twice a year the priests visit each village in the parish," and "Mass is said in one house in each village and all the villagers gather into that house to hear Mass and confess their sins." Over and over, O'Flaherty has as his subject matter the social phenomena of western life, from the viewpoint of the ordinary peasant living it, rather than from that of the outsider looking in from above or beyond. "The Mountain Tavern," which presents the devastation of an area caught between two uncaring armies during the Troubles, is a good example of where O'Flaherty's populist sympathies lie. As the best of the portrayers in English of ordinary Irish life on the land, O'Flaherty is more understandable to non-Irish readers than Daniel Corkery and Standish O'Grady, and more sheerly interesting than Brinsley McNamara and Bryan MacMahon. Specifically, his skill in rendering country matters won O'Flaherty the admiration of both O'Connor and O'Faolain.[6]

An early story, "The Fairy Goose" (1926), reflects a typical O'Flaherty defense of a folk belief that has been denounced as heresy. The enchanted goose is supposed by the superstitious to be a good fairy, but it is cruelly stoned to death by vandals acting on the priest's wishes. The death connotes the eradication of magic in the country. After Mary Wiggins curses "the village, the priest, and all mankind," O'Flaherty ends the story with a statement about what has been lost:

> ... it appeared that her blasphemous prayer took some effect at least. Although giants did not war in the heavens and cows did not give birth to fishes, it is certain that from

> that day the natives of that village are quarrelsome drunk-
> ards who fear God but do not love one another. And the old
> woman is again collecting followers from among the wives
> of the drunkards. These women maintain that the only
> time in the history of their generation that there was peace
> and harmony in the village was during the time that the
> fairy goose was loved by the people.

The Cathleen-like "old woman" who is again "collecting followers" is clearly O'Flaherty's heroine, and the story pits her generosity of feeling against repression, privilege, and pietism. He persevered in arguing on the side of magic and superstitition in an analoguous story twenty-six years later when he published "The Enchanted Water" in *The Yale Review*, a story which has associations with the tale of the Children of Lir. O'Flaherty's wide use of folk elements constitutes yet another aspect of the romantic nature of his short stories, an aspect that honors Yeats's and AE's often expressed desire for the imminent return of the Celtic gods.

From "Spring Sowing" (1942) through "Two Lovely Beasts" (1946) and after, the best of O'Flaherty's stories prove to be also the most representative. "Spring Sowing" equates the energy and promise of a newly married couple with the immemorial forces set stirring by the fecundation of the earth in the spring. As in Stravinsky's *Rite of Spring*, everything strains: the sky looks "as if it were going to burst in order to give birth to the sun." Poised against the exultant rhythms of promise in the foreground is Mary's discordant knowledge that this backbreaking labor will be exacted from her and her husband right to the mouth of the grave, that she and Martin are now integral with the sidereal flow of life and death. A sort of hymn to the dignifying process of human effort and depletion, the story bespeaks the emergence of a young writer of unusual maturity and power. This same maturity informs "Going Into Exile" (1924), in which, for the departing children, the hurt and fear of emigrating are balanced by the excitement of new prospects. The main virtues of the story are its controlled yet emotional writing and its sensitivity to the melange of feelings experienced by the parents and their children. In the final lines, the mother needs the social strength of Synge's Maurya in *Riders to the Sea* to absorb the realization that her loving Mary and Michael have been exchanged for the abstractions of time and patience:

> She looked wildly down the road with dilated nostrils, her
> bosom heaving. But there was nobody in sight. Nobody

replied. There was a crooked stretch of limestone road,
surrounded by grey crags that were scorched by the sun.
The road ended in a hill and then dropped out of sight. The
hot July day was silent. Listening foolishly for an answer-
ing cry, the mother imagined she could hear the crags
simmering under the hot rays of the sun. It was something
in her head that was singing.

The two old women led her back into the kitchen.
"There is nothing that time will not cure," said one. "Yes,
time and patience," said the other.

"The Conger Eel" (1924) succeeds nicely in enlisting the reader's
support for the eel's attempt to escape and in activating the reader's
dislike for the fishermen bent on killing it. We struggle along with the
snaky fish as it fights to regain the water: "His snout dipped into the
sea. With an immense shiver, he glided away, straight down, down
to the depths, down like an arrow, until he reached the dark, weed-
covered rocks at the bottom." Here, as in many of his early stories,
O'Flaherty pictures men as faceless murderers vexing an animal
kingdom that observes a peremptory but more honorable natural
balance. In general, he takes a programmatic and simple view of
things: in his first volumes, when men are seen in an unindividuated
group, they are usually predatory; when O'Flaherty focuses in on
selected specimens of the group, his sympathy dilates along with his
lens. Just as simply, women are usually sources of compassion, as we
just saw in the quotation from *Going Into Exile*. Complexity, irony, and
ambivalence do not appear routinely in his short work until his fourth
volume of stories, *Two Lovely Beasts* (1948), which gathered together
twenty new stories largely written during the years of World War II
that O'Flaherty spent in Connecticut.

Two other animal stories match *The Conger Eel* in excitement,
empathy for endangered nature, and suspense: "The Wild Goat's Kid"
(1925) and "The Wounded Cormorant" (1925). The wild goat embod-
ies another version of the good mother theme, but she is a much better
example of O'Flaherty's other staple character, the outcast or outsider
who goes it alone: "She had wandered too far away from her master's
village . . . So that she became a wild one of the cliffs. . . ." The story
is of an Eden invaded by a prowling dog. The fight over the kid
between the goat and the dog—defensive female and male assailant—
offers a blood-stirring sample of O'Flaherty's flair for action-writing,
a tempo which is put aside when Eden is again established. In the
ending, violence and sentiment blend with justice and peace:

But she was ferocious now. As she wriggled to her feet
beside the rolling dog that gripped her flank, she wrenched
herself around and gored him savagely in the belly. He
yelled and loosened his hold. She rose on her hind legs in
a flash, and with a snort she gored him again. Her sharp,
pointed horns penetrated his side between the ribs. He
gasped and shook his four feet in the air. Then she
pounded on him with her forefeet, beating his prostate
body furiously. Her little hoofs pattered with tremendous
speed for almost a minute. She beat him blindly, without
looking at him . . .

　　Night passed into a glorious dawn that came over a
rippling sea from the east. A wild, sweet dawn scented
with dew and the many perfumes of the germinating earth.
The sleepy sun rose brooding from the sea, golden and soft,
searching far horizons with its concave shafts of light. The
dawn was still. Still and soft and pure.

The dog, himself an outsider from the human community, serves as an
agent of it, no doubt dispatched by a farmer to round up stray sheep
or goats on the mountainside. The wild goat's slaying of him is an act
of purification, the same subject developed by O'Flaherty in "The
Wounded Cormorant" (1925). Here the disabled bird is killed by its
own kind which will not suffer parasites. Coincidentally, the stone
that strikes and breaks the cormorant's leg is jarred loose from the crag
above the bird by a frightened goat. From the moment of the
wounding, the bird's doom is ordained. Its fellows fall upon it fiercely,
"tearing at its body with their beaks, plucking out its black feathers and
rooting it about with their feet . . . and, dragging it to the brink of the
ledge, they hurled it down."

　　"The Tent" (1925) takes up the subject of hospitality abused,
abused by ex-Sergeant-Major Carney who insults his tinker hosts
when he mentions that he feels demeaned by having to walk the roads.
Carney is an intruder in the tinker camp from the officious world; the
tinker and his two women are "cut off from the mass of society,"
outsiders living still in a state of nature. After Carney commits the
supercilious man's error of treating the tinkers as if they were social
inferiors, he ends up pitched out into the night by the infuriated tinker
for trifling with one of his women. "Fair play," pleads the retreating
Carney, invoking one of the shibboleths of his recent imperial employ-
ers. The earmark of this story is subtlety. O'Flaherty leaves the tinker's
inner reactions and sense of horror for the reader to infer. The story
remains understated until Carney tramps off toward Roundwood

crying out righteously, "God Almighty!" and crossing himself. The unorthodox and appealing code by which the taciturn tinker lives is indicated by his actions. O'Flaherty's sympathy for his sleazy and defiant way of life looks forward to Brian Moore's in *The Feast of Lupercal*. Even in their dirt and dissipation, the tinker and his women have more real dignity than the wretched Carney.

"Two Lovely Beasts" (1946) is an example of the man-of-independence story, and one of O'Flaherty's longest. After recounting the ups and downs of Colm Derrane's struggle to achieve fortune and status, during which Derrane climbs from farmer to bourgeois, O'Flaherty slyly questions the cost to Derrane and his wife of their "rise." The people of the village envy them, and the town scourge, Gorum, whips us a tirade about new exploiters who "are taking all our lovely beasts across the sea to fill the bellies of pagans." The word "our" in the mouth of the feckless Gorum drips with irony. Ultimately, we detect that the two lovely beasts of the title are not really the calves that Colm Derrane and his wife have sacrificed so much to raise; rather, they are themselves who have grown "cold and resolute and ruthless" in spiting the villagers. The observation that idealism takes a toll on one's humanity, may even make one a fanatic, introduces a viewpoint that continued through *Two Lovely Beasts* to "Galway Bay" at the very end.[7] "Galway Bay" (1939) tells of a snappish eighty-year-old man, disappointed with life and recovering from an argument with his modern-minded daughter, who travels by steamer to Galway with his cow, which he intends to sell in order to purchase his coffin and to order some Masses said after his death. It is a beautiful, bittersweet story of old age, of Tom O'Donnell's will and senses in decline, of the last of the old breed of Aran men. Tom is puzzled and disappointed by the new things he sees: women in trousers, an ocean-going liner, islandmen domesticated by life in the town. Regretting having quarreled with his daughter, he marches off the steamer and up the lonely road with the cow, which is as decrepit as himself: "He walked beside her with downcast head, one hand on his high hip-bone, the other leaning heavily on his stick." For this touching old man who still treasures his "spunk," everything is gone or going, and he can no longer apprehend the beauty of the bay he once knew so well. All of the sadness of aging is here, the ghostly sense of glories past. With "Lovers" it is O'Flaherty's best story of the old.

"The Blow" (1954) contrasts two generations as a father and son go to purchase a litter of pigs from a large farm. The father has become

a greedy hotel-keeper, "Almost . . . a complete savage," to whom the
pigs are simply more chattels to be acquired. To his son Neidin they
are creatures of vital beauty: "There was far more depth of understanding in [his eyes] already than in those of his father; understanding and wonder and suffering." Three blows in the course of the story
attest to the insensitivity of Neidin's father. The first blow is that given
by the boar to a pen door that separates him from the sow: "Oh, you
devil," says Neidin, "there was a blow for you." He dislikes confining
the animals, unlike his father, who believes in commercial mating.
The second blow comes when the sow accidentally strikes her weakling piglet. To the father, the sow is correcting and rebuking the
piglet's unaggressiveness by this action; to Neidin, she is showing her
regret that the weakling cannot find a place at her teats. The father
shouts that the sow hit the piglet on purpose, because that is "how it
is in the world. There is neither pity nor mercy, among people as well
as among animals, bad or good, for the weak or the cowardly." To
veteran readers of O'Flaherty, the father merely voices truths reflected
in his work since "The Seal" and "The Wounded Cormorant." But the
third blow, administered to Neidin by his father in retribution for
Neidin's siding with the weakling piglet, "banishes from his consciousness everything that pertained to the divinity of his nature."
Neidin's godly love of life "is knocked out of him" and "pride and
contempt" enter in, until the sow overtly summons its weakling to
nurse. Then "love . . . returned to the world," and Neidin can decently
cry and feel affection for his boorish father. Chastened in turn by his
son's display of feeling, the father for once softens toward him.
Clearly, the story marks a softening of O'Flaherty himself, a willing-
ness to acknowledge in human animals the existence of transforming
virtues such as mercy and pity, which can alter behavior for the better.[8]
This appealing point of view indicates O'Flaherty's mellowing in later
life. At the same time, "The Blow" retains his life-long attitude that
earthly good resides mainly in animals and old people and children.

Notes

[1] Quoted in *Liam O'Flaherty* by James H. O'Brien (Lewisburg, PA: Bucknell University Press, 1973) 23.

[2] Readers will find most of O'Flaherty's best short stories in these two collected hard-cover editions: *The Short Stories of Liam O'Flaherty* (London: Jonathan Cape, 1937) and *The Stories of Liam O'Flaherty*, Introd. by Vivian Mercier (New York: Devin-Adair, 1956).

[3] As was the case with Sean O'Faolain, a major influence on O'Flaherty in his younger years was the English writer and editor Edward Garnett, who was himself a personal friend of Lawrence and Conrad and whose wife, Constance, was the English translator of Dostoievski.

[4] This phrase serves as the title for one of O'Flaherty's autobiographies: *Shame the Devil* (London: Grayson and Grayson, 1934).

[5] A. A. Kelly, Introduction, in Liam O'Flaherty's *The Pedlar's Revenge and Other Stories* (Dublin: The Wolfhound Press, 1976) 10.

[6] See Frank O'Connor, "A Good Short Story Must Be News" *The New York Times Book Review*, I (June 10, 1956), 20 and Sean O'Faolain, "Don Quixote O'Flaherty," *The Bell*, II (June, 1941), 28-36. O'Connor mentions O'Flaherty's special mastery in describing the instinctual life of his characters and quotes an old Munster woman telling him that "I do be lighting candles for Liam O'Flaherty." O'Faolain's assessment is similar: " . . . one has the feeling that O'Flaherty has his ear to the earth, listening carefully" (35).

[7] Actually, O'Flaherty first published "Galway Bay" in 1939 and "Two Lovely Beasts" in 1946; the order in which the stories are placed in "Two Lovely Beasts" reverses the order of composition.

[8] Vivian Mercier, too, believes that "The Blow" "shows the compassion of O'Flaherty's later stories." *Great Irish Short Stories* (New York: Dell Publishing Co., 1964) 237.

Chapter Five

All Things Known: Mary Lavin

I. Mary Lavin is unexcludable in any list of Irish short story masters from the origins of the form to now. Only half a generation younger than O'Connor, O'Faolain, and O'Flaherty, she has had much greater difficulty achieving a niche like theirs along the Anglo-American axis. Although the subject of three book-length studies and a sheaf of articles and introductions, all of them adulatory almost without cavil, her international reputation remains immobilized in the cubbyhole assigned it by V. S. Pritchett when he placed her in the company of "Leskov, Aksakov or Shchredin; not of Turgenev or Tolstoy."[1] This is a considerable unfairness.

Commentators take for granted that Lavin writes stories about only a small number of situations: the pain of widowhood, daughter-raising, the possibility and need of a revived love-life, nasty families, aging and dying. Actually, her stories are of a very bountiful number of sorts and types, showing a never-resting habit of experimentation that works against her displaying the representative fingerprint, the single essence of her three great confreres. The quality of experimentation persistently characterizes her collected stories, occasionally leading her into such faults as excessive length, plot confusions, and irresolute conclusions but also providing her with so generous a range of character types and settings and moods and stylistic voices that she bridges the whole spectrum of the Irish short story from Joycean mandarinism to the rustic matters and manners of the anecdotal story-teller.

I propose to look at three major aspects of her stories, each subdividing in two, and then to examine the workings of a typical Lavin story ("A Memory"), one that I believe summarizes her teeming powers. The first aspect has to do with her major themes of paralysis and entrapment and their indebtedness to Joyce's *Dubliners*. In the second part, I take note of her world view, or mainly those modalities of it which hold that at the center of human joy is sadness, and that human perception is largely controlled by protective self-delusion.

Thirdly, Lavin's artistic technique is analyzed and its principal polarities discussed.

Asked for "influences" in a 1967 interview, Lavin cited James Joyce, along with Chekhov, Turgenev, Flaubert, Lawrence, Tolstoy, and James, as producers of the literature she had "read" as an apprentice writer as distinct from that of other writers to whom she "owed most," namely, Edith Wharton, George Sand, and "especially" Sarah Orne Jewett.[2] Of those mentioned, the writers who seem closest to the nerve and pulse of her work are Joyce and James. From the first she took a major facet of her subject matter; her method of presentation developed along lines that we associate with the second.

How else can we explain the constantly iterated presence in her stories of borrowings from "Eveline," "A Painful Case," and "The Boarding House," or her lifelong employment of expansive and all-seeing first- and third-person Jamesian narrators? The influence of Joyce concerns me initially, as it must have the young Ph.D. candidate at University College Dublin at the time that Joyce's popular reputation was mounting in the 'Thirties. The well-known emphasis on paralysis in *Dubliners* is taken over in so many stories that it becomes one of Lavins's chief themes, manifesting her view of life's condition as one of perpetual conflict. One of Lavin's most customary methods of working, especially in her early work, is to offer "sequels" to the proto-stories of Joyce, and to do so in a lambent psychological style that by its trueness makes a further scrutiny of the malaise of Eveline and Little Chandler and Bob Doran endurable. Many of her stories read as natural completions of ones "outlined" by Joyce.

Thus in the early story "At Sallygap," Eveline-like Manny, lured back down the gangplank in Dublin harbor from which he was escaping to Paris with his musician pals, has hardened over the years of marriage since then into a lifeless drudge, so meek and obliging that his wife almost wishes that he had the spirit to become a drunkard or wife-beater. But "he was the same always . . . she tried from time to time to break the strength of his weakness, and she fought against his kindness as if it were her enemy. And so, in an obscure way, it was." The paradoxes of strength in weakness and of kindness as an enemy are typical features of Lavin's crystalline perception in a story that explores the effects of causes first elicited by Joyce.

It is the woman's turn to exhibit the same kind of petrified unresponsiveness in "The Cuckoo-Spit." When walking with her young suitor, Vera shudders with revulsion when the seminal white

fluid of the gadabout cuckoo bird touches her hand. She can see only
the snake in the garden, actually "a pale, sickly-yellow aphis," crawl-
ing on her hand, and shake it off violently. One recalls Emily Sinico's
"crossing the line" to touch Mr. James Duffy and his ultimate expulsion from the garden-park at the end of "A Painful Case." "Can there
be friendship between a man and a woman?" the youthful swain in
Lavin's story asks, and is told: "Friendship is so exacting. Perhaps that
is why [love and friendship] can never exist at the same time."[5] Here
in clouds of dreamy dialogue is Lavin's ingenious inversion of the
conundrum voiced by Joyce's Mr. Duffy that "friendship between man
and woman is impossible because there must be sexual intercourse."[3]

Psychological blockage of this type overcomes a number of
Lavin characters. To name just a few: Rose Darker in "A Gentle Soul,"
whose overweening father prevents her escape to Australia; the
milktoast pursuer of the title character in "Posy"; Mary, who feels "a
sudden terrible aimlessness descend upon herself like physical paralysis," in "In a Cafe"; the father-fixated and Australia-denied Vera in
"One Summer"; or the negated and nameless heroine in "Assigh" who
is crippled by a beating her father gave her for talking to a young
man—all are victims of the conflict that Lavin habitually delineates
between centripetal duty and centrifugal impulse, usually that of love.

It is societal pressure, or course, that validates responsibility's
victory over impulse. Over and over, human action in Lavin's stories
is dictated by what "they," or the town, or communal opinion, or
gossip, or fear of gossip, will say or think. There is also a complemen-
tary theme to the Joycean one of paralysis, which is the equally Joycean
one of entrapment. In "The Convert," a sensitive young man is trapped
into a life as a shopkeeper by a combination of his wife's scheming and
the conventional expectations of the provincial community. Lavin
continually awakens the shopkeeper Elgar's awareness of what his
diminished self looks like by having him glance into a mirror, or view
snapshots, or contemplate his lookalike daughter Birdie. The story
rings with doubleness as Lavin shows the horror and boredom of a
respectable life, the conversion of Elgar putatively to Catholicism but
actually to emasculation.

In point of fact we know what happened to Joyce's Bob Doran
after he married Polly in "The Boarding House" because we see him in
a state of alcoholic delirium in *Ulysses*. But Lavin has her own version
of that story's denouement entitled "A Woman Friend," in which a
physician who is for a time accused by a board of inquiry ("them"

again) of falling asleep on duty foolishly blurts out a marriage proposal to a homely, inferior, designedly sympathetic girl named Bina.
Her mother keeps a small hotel where he once was taken in, in two
senses. The pastiche of Joyce is clearly signaled in the opening lines of
the story by the impersonal narrator's assurance that "No blame had
attached to him at all" and in the concluding lines which state that the
incident "was only a little cloud that blew up in a clear sky." The
physician's mental thickness in being unable to fully register the cost
of his impetuous proposal is ironically given in his stream of consciousness: "If he had kept his head he would have known that
everything would be all right. . . . And now everything would be the
same as ever—only for Bina." The physician insists, especially to
himself, that he has not been victimized because he wants to be
admired for his goodness and beheld as faultless. Thus, like Doran, he
does the "proper" thing when Bina, in her raggedy kimono, laves him
with sympathy.

One final version of what might be called Lavin's post-Eveline/
Chandler/Doran theme should be momentarily mentioned, namely
the story entitled "Eterna" which appeared in *The New Yorker* in 1976.
The story offers another examination of the effects of a bad marriage
on the human spirit, this time in the case of a physician whose interest
in art is trivialized by his dull, materialistic wife. The physician's slow
suffocation first emulates and then offers a conclusion to the quandary
of Little Chandler in "A Little Cloud." Few writers have known as well
as Lavin how to extract the rich juice from the windfalls Joyce left
scattered in *Dubliners*. However, there is a difference in setting
between Lavin's development of the theme of paralysis and entrapment and Joyce's: Lavin's stories avoid an explicit Irish ambience and
thus her focus is not socio-political but universal. Her persistent use
of this theme accommodates itself within a general statement about
the natural strife and conflict of life. Let us turn to that general
statement.

II. There is a distinctly lugubrious note struck in the plot and
the setting of many Lavin stories, especially in those of her early and
middle periods. Cemeteries abound, and there is a general sense that
the good cheer of life in the past is being sullied by the demoralizing
disintegration of the present. Nostalgia not only isn't what it used to

be but, when we learn the truth about the past, we see that it never was. A succession of women who symbolically mutilate and kill males issues forth across her pages in stories like "The Patriot Son," "The Widow's Son," "A Cup of Tea," "A Happy Death," and "The Little Prince." They contain a proliferation of anti-Cathleens launched on an inexorable sexist campaign of misanthropy, and Lavin consistently condemns them. The spiritless, missing father, or Nobadaddy, of Joyce is replaced by the victim as outcast in Lavin, and the women who demean and dismiss their men end up themselves pitiful and demented. A story called "The Little Prince," in which an exiled brother in Boston totally ignores his Irish family and nationality until the sister who drove him out is gutted with guilt, is a good synedoche for this tendency in her work.

Clearly, Lavin projects in her stories the so-called tragic sense of life, the acceptance of mankind's natural proclivity for defeat despite resistance. Important art is made from this predisposition by making palpable the bittersweet beauty and worth of life. The attesting is a way of overcoming, as writers since at least the Roman poets have said, a way of using beautiful means to vanquish grim ends.

In a slightly different way, Mary Lavin's stories often offer what might be called beautiful moments that are extirpated by life's essential sadness. Consider the dark humor of "The Cemetery in the Demesne" by way of illustration. The loquacious and buoyant carter is brought low by his meeting with the poor lady at the gate lodge and the news of her sick child—it seems that for almost the first time human sadness has intruded traumatically on his brute cheerfulness and left him thoughtful and inarticulate. This is precisely what Lavin's best stories do to us all: "... the day's events fell into place and formed a picture—the still, white child and the damp graveyard, and the furtive rat and the rainy funerals, and the fierce blue eyes of the lodgekeeper's wife." In the midst of the quagmire, images of hopelessness forever gather.

In "Sunday Brings Sunday," Mona counts out her life in relentless week-long units, sexually ignorant and probably pregnant, clinging to her one joyful memory of the luckless Jimmy, fated to become an old hag like the crazed beldam who announces doom in the chapel yard. In Lavin's world, the triumphant instant stands in the center and then is swept away. In "The Long Ago," Hallie is the only unmarried one of three close friends. After her soulmates are widowed, she

attempts to comfort them but makes the crucial social blunder of
declaring that the three old chums, now unencumbered, can be
together again. Her hopeful but indelicate nostalgia is quickly denounced by the affronted widows. In another tale of solemn setting,
"A Visit to the Cemetery," which has been praised as "a little masterpiece,"[4] the two young girls in the end lock up behind them the old
cemetery of their ancestors which will not claim them—they derive
contentment from anticipating their occupancy of the parish's brand-
new cemetery. The old and new cemeteries, the past and the future,
one revered and the other promising, are both but cemeteries—their
contentment is illusory.

Perhaps the best story on this sort of theme or world-view is "A
Cup of Tea." The mother's happy anticipation of her daughter's return
is spoiled when the girl arrives and visits her reclusive father while the
jealous mother waits downstairs and spoils the tea. Pathetically, the
mother cannot stop herself from starting a savage argument with the
daughter. In the bedroom, the daughter examines her face in the
mirror and, thinking of the photograph in the hallway of her father
when young, inspects a third image, one which she takes from her
suitcase:

> It was the photograph of another young man, also straight
> and also stiff, with serious eyes and a stern look, because
> these are the attributes which young men wish to appear to
> possess when they have their pictures taken. Sophie stared
> at the photograph, and then she ran to the mirror and
> stared at her own face. But she had not learned anything
> by looking at either face, for she sighed and got into bed.

There is in this passage, of course, a lovely evocation of the young girl's
blissful ignorance of time's changes. But, more importantly, the
reader has been made aware of the evanescence of the common lot.
How artfully Lavin suggests the image of Sophie's parents when they
were young, their one-time likeness to Sophie and her young man, and
the inevitable universal degeneration into domestic division and
death.

Lavin's vision, then, is fixed on the impending darkness, the
crack in the teacup that anticipates death. Witness the postulate Sister
Veronica washing the expensive gloves that her worldly sister has
accidentally left behind on the day of Veronica's First Vows in "Cham-
ois Gloves"—they contrast with the life of denial that she has chosen,
and she leaves them wistfully before "retiring." A clever symbol in a

less-good story is the train travelled on by the middle-aged honey-
mooners in "Heart of Gold." Lucy has finally married Sam after he has
spent years married to a woman who unscrupulously took him away
from Lucy. On the train, his unremitting reminiscences of his first wife
so nauseate Lucy that she considers suicide. Her ranging through the
various compartments of the train hints at the extent of their psychic
separation,[5] before she returns to her chastened and amorous husband
in their own private compartment. But the reader knows that Lucy has
unwittingly involved herself in a ghostly *menage à trois* that will
include Sam's departed first wife.

If it is customary for Lavin's protagonists to see joy or the
possibility of joy put to rout, she has devised for them a defense
mechanism that works for at least a short time, namely some type of
grand vision or illusion. That happiness can be held onto only by
distorting reality is a common belief of her characters who often do so
obsessively. A few hasty examples of this phenomenon should
include that of the progressively more self-deceived Ella in "A Happy
Death" who announces her intention to bestow ever-larger presents
on her penniless, dying husband though she in actuality has hastened
his demise by many years of neglect: "Like the bench in front of the
house, like the cottage with the three rooms, like the grapes, the
oranges, the books of poetry with the gold edges, now it was eternal
salvation she wanted for him." "A Happy Death" is a mordantly funny
story, as is a slyer one named "The Small Bequest" in which a rich old
lady's companion of many years is cut off in her will but refuses to
acknowledge the snub. It seems that rich Miss Tate has secretly
resented the hireling Miss Blodgett's assumption of equality, of being
one of the family, while Miss Blodgett's defense in rejection is an iron
curtain of unruffled equanimity. This story of decorousness, of which
more will be said later, is told with the most prodigious skill and irony
of presentation. The will-o'-the-wisp narrative pivots on the revela-
tions of a first-person narrator of Jamesian subtlety, while Emma
Blodgett comes to suggest a facetious version of bovine, uncon-
sciously vulgar Emma Bovary. Once again, the emphasis is on heroic
and salutary self-delusion.

The habit of "mixing up sentiment and mockery" until they
produce " a kind of cheating" obsesses the villainess of "Frail Vessel"
and is a central tendency of Lavin's characters. The weakling Adolphus Carmody routinely begs from others and is forced to leave town
by his sister-in-law Bedelia after an act of embezzlement. Bedelia had

intended to use her sister (and Adolphus's wife) Liddy Carmody as a house servant of herself and her husband; now with Adolphus gone she will have to support Liddy's unborn child and, as family head, endure Liddy's newly besmirched reputation. Each sister has her own overweening obsession: Liddy is the height of witless dependency and Bedelia of insensitivity; Liddy is bereft of a sense of blame or responsibility as Bedelia is of sympathy or forgiveness. Here there is to be found again the Lavin formula of a moment of obsessed, manic behavior deriving from a self-deceiving grand passion. In another typical tale, a maniacal seminarian in "The Great Wave" refuses to cut away the bulging fish nets as a tidal wave strikes lethally at all the surrounding boats and kills all the inhabitants of his village. "I'll not let go this net, not if it pulls me down to hell," he shouts. Faint echoes of *Moby Dick* and *Riders to the Sea* intrude on this story which invades the *métier* of Liam O'Flaherty right down to "the solitary oar" that protrudes from the terrible wall of water. But the story finally adheres to the Lavin mode: the seminarian loses his faith, murders it in fact through his greed and suicidal need to show his virility. As elsewhere, obsession is the precondition of self-destruction.

We should not abandon the typical Lavin theme of grand delusion without quickly mentioning two of her finest stories which exemplify it marvelously, "One Evening" and "Trastevere." In the first, a young boy bicycles home on an evening like any other to find his father sitting outside the house in his car and asserting that he has just killed the boy's mother. Inside, he finds the mother quite alive but distracted from making the lad's dinner by a desire to play the father's favorite song on the piano which she has not touched for years. Estranged and ignored, the boy rides away leaving each dazed and divided parent to cultivate his and her private delusion, the father's of his infuriating wife being punished and banished, and the mother's of her tyrannous husband as a young lover once again.

"Trastevere" is equally startling and powerful. It concerns the sudden news given to Mrs. Traske (a favorite stand-in of Lavin's for herself) of the suicide in Rome of a young and assertive woman met by Mrs. Traske at a writers' conference the summer before. As Mrs. Traske reviews the summer meeting, she gradually detects that Della's apparent strength was only a role she played in supporting two artistic men, her husband and his friend, who encourage her sacrificial mothering while she burns herself out in their service. "Was it possible," Mrs Traske asks herself, "that Della wasn't strong at all?" In the end, the shattering knowledge of Della's self-slaughter and of her true character impels Mrs. Traske to renounce for good the cultivation of self-deceit.

This latter story of slow truth filtering through upon reflection resembles the slowly emerging figure-in-the-carpet technique of Henry James and of his acolytes Edith Wharton (especially as used in "Roman Fever") and Sarah Orne Jewett. It is time to consider some of the earmarks of Lavin's technique.

III. The stories of Mary Lavin are notable for their finesse in handling the comedy-of-manners material that we associate with writers like Austen, Trollope, Flaubert, and James. The family is her natural setting, the social cockpit where sentiment and mockery compete most overtly. She has written forthrightly humorous stories such as "The Long Holidays," "My Vocation," and "A Pure Accident," but the larger sense of the human comedy is her principal vein: girls growing up, the winning of husbands, the slow decay of love, the end of youthful ideals, the dependency of aged parents. Her stories are now and then allegorical maps that graph the behavior of one quintessential family that suggests all others, and they are occasionally domestic fables that point a moral; more frequently they are animated by symbolic details that are pungent and give authority to her feel for the domestic scene.

Among her best and most typical stories of the comedy-of-manners sort should be counted "The Small Bequest," "In the Middle of the Field," "Happiness," "A Single Lady," "The Lost Child," "A Mug of Water," and "Senility."

The first of these has been mentioned briefly already but is worthy of further attention because of its high wit and riddling power. Miss Blodgett, the inherently vulgar companion to the dowager Miss Tate, takes the unwarranted liberty of referring to her benefactress as "Aunt Adeline." When she dies, Miss Tate cuts Miss Blodgett from her will and showers her largesse on the docile Hetty who knows her place as a servant. But, one wonders, doesn't Emma Blodgett *know* that her familiar approaches to Miss Tate are giving offense, and isn't her pleasure in making bold with the high and mighty her irresistible boon for the likelihood of disinheritance?

Surely Lavin uses Emma Blodgett to strike back on all of our behalves against the oppressions of caste. And Blodgett's refusal to admit disappointment after she is rejected in the will becomes her source of secret mirth and a proof to us of her pride and unwillingness to be subjugated, and so of her ultimate victory. Lavin sows the story with delicate hints of pride and prejudice and relates the whole wonderful battle through the eyes of an all-noticing neighbor who registers seismically each nuance of Miss Tate's annoyance but is blind and dumb to the intentions of Miss Blodgett. Over and over the narrator observes Miss Tate's "arrows" of innuendo loosed at the amiable Blodgett, and she tells us of the wicked old lady's will in which Miss Tate leaves a large sum to "my fond *niece*, Emma" a sum which is legally uninheritable as Miss Tate well knew. But the narrator's judgment that Miss Blodgett is "stupid" is not to be our judgment. There is lively irony in this most skillful story with its gradual disclosures and exquisite sensibilities.

"In the Middle of the Field" is the title story of a 1966 collection dedicated to "Michael Scott, S. J." who was soon after laicized and became Mary Lavin's second husband. She herself in 1966 was "in the middle of the field" of her life and career, as is her unnamed, widowed heroine who in a night-time scene confronts the hired man, Bartley Crossen, who has come to "cut her field" and "top her land." As the scene progresses, it emits gradually intensifying sexual vibrations. In time, the nocturnal meeting becomes for each a battle for dominance done not as a Lawrencian Armageddon but with a kind of teasing enjoyment on the part of the widow and of Lavin. Crossen is eventually rejected—after trying ineptly for "a little kiss," the widow puts him to flight by invoking the name of his first wife which is probably the only shibboleth strong enough to cool his ardor. Crossen doesn't see but the reader does that he is pursuing his first wife's ghost in making advances upon the widow, while the widow is probing the extent of her own regained strength—there is in the story a layer of "knitting together" imagery that applies to both her and Crossen. Lavin catches beautifully the complicated etiquette of the friendly but serious fields of middle-aged sexual strife, an area of expertise for only a few writers.

Manners are similarly central in "Happiness," another story of a widow named Vera who has three young daughters to raise. The title is facetious—for Vera happiness is something wrested from the world only by bashing it with a bloody club. Lavin lovingly records Vera's never-ending anxiety as she rears her children, lays her mother to rest, and keeps herself alive by serving others. What emerges most impressively in the story is the abundance of Lavin's moral passion, her ability to dramatize the ennobling virtues of forebearance, tenacity, humor, self-sacrifice, sensitivity, compassion, and love, all of which Vera manifests and teaches her daughters with the aid of Father Hugh, the family's longtime friend. But the happiness of pleasure eludes Vera herself who in the extremity of her concern for others knows only the happiness of responsibility well discharged.

Surely this dutiful kind of happiness is integral to the enigma of motherhood where it weights down joyful inclinations with the urden of authority. For Vera, every aspect of life is hard-won, anxious; she has been "beset by life, like other parents? and forced to weather "the onslaughts that were made upon our happiness!" Finally, her daughters grown and married, she herself nearing death, Vera cries out that she can't face the journey ahead, a plaint that triggers a most poignant and affecting conclusion. Vera's daughter Bea speaks the *coup de grâce*:

> 'It's all right, Mother. You don't *have* to face it! It's over!' Then she who had so fiercely forbade Father Hugh to do so blurted out the truth. 'You've finished with this world, Mother," she said, and, confident that her tidings were joyous, her voice was strong.
> Mother made the last effort of her life and grasped at Bea's meaning. She let out a sigh and, closing her eyes, she sank back, and this time her head sank so deep into the pillow that it would have been dented had it been a pillow of stone.

Apparently Vera carries worry and effort with her even into the afterworld in a scene rich in sad humor.

It is Lavin's characteristic power to detect the sad humor at the heart of families and of final things. One is reminded of her use of a similarly rueful note in "A Single Lady" in which an elderly man flirts with a gold-digging servant girl until his forty-year-old daughter Isabel tries to open his eyes to his error by relating one night at the fireplace to her father and the servant girl a parable of another old man who made a fool of himself over a plotting temptress. Isabel winds up her story by saying warningly of the temptress: "She got what she wanted." But the servant girl's comeback tops her warning: "*He* got what he wanted, too, didn't he?"[23]

Often Lavin's stories move outward from an expected develop

ment to larger social and human implications, which is the stock-in-trade of the writer of manners. A good example of this proclivity is to be seen in "The Lost Child" in which a pregnant woman just converted to Catholicism loses her foetus through massive overwork and ends up in a sickbed surrounded by her sister, her husband, and the converting priest who makes eyes at the sister. Ambivalence clusters about the bed as one tries to sort out the relationship between husband and wife, unborn child and its possibly murderous mother, the woman and the priest of her new religion, and the priest and his vow of celibacy. A novel seems needed to straighten it all out. Lavin exemplifies in her stories that people in love often find one another bizarre and full of frightening differentnesses from oneself.

This is the comic turn that "The Mug of Water" exploits when a young physician keeps dragging his bewildered wife into increasingly scary archeological explorations. Another story that widens out as it proceeds is the touchingly funny one entitled "Senility" in which a mother and daughter are locked together by love while being driven apart by aging. The story might have been better called "Incontinence," because it focuses on the mother's mortifying bed-wetting and, more importantly, on the slow break-up between the two generations. The mother is riven between self-reliance and dependency, and the daughter Laura between her loyalty to her mother and to her husband. "Lord, Lord, don't make it too hard on me," prays the mother, and then amends her prayer: "Don't make it too hard on Laura, I mean."

Into the widening ripples of nuance that typify her stories, Lavin often introduces symbolic details and suggestive terms that expand the story's social, familial, and personal implications. These small profusions of craft come as adornments to her intimate and realistic style and her many-toned narrative voice. Maybe her best-known symbol is the violin in "At Sallygap" that is thrown from the boat Manny Ryan was to take to Paris and a life of music and freedom but which smashes at his feet on the "iron stumps" of the dock.[6] Manny now lives "past the Gaiety" and "within a stone's throw of thePillar," details which suggest his victimization in marriage to Annie. His cold dinner is saved in a doily of congealed grease after his long walk home from the hills in the dead of night, a tableau that reminds us of his impotency and symbolic death. The miserable Manny thinks of Annie's green eyes, formerly hopeful, now jealous of other women who have been given more virile lovers—Manny associates the color with the dirty water of Dunlaoghaire pier, his lost medium of escape.

Water has the same negative-but-once-positive value in "The Sand Castle" in which three children collaborate with the sea to build their edifice but are motivated to destroy it before the incoming tide can. The story has the restless energy and vital deeps of the sea itself.

Although one can only theorize as to what the three children— two wanting to be king and queen of the castle while making their freckled playmate a servant—stand for in a mock-epic interpretation of the story, the futile but stimulating and necessary making of the castle is reminiscent of the tales of Sisyphus and Tantalus as well as a vehicle for Lavin's pronouncement son the work of the artist and the nature of art. Thus, English-seeming John creates from tin-foil a moat which seems more utile and durable than water, and he endows the castle with doors and windows of such realness that the Irish-seeming Alexander can only mutter in awe the word "Gosh!" The sound of this word is duplicated perfectly by the "thin white lips" of the sea running up the shingle behind him. The art-*versus*-nature icon posited by the story gives way in the end to an explicit aesthetic declaration by the author: "When the artist first begins to shape his creation he is filled with a pride in himself and cannot bear to think that any hand but his could shape the perfection of the dream behind his brain, but as the dream emerges into a tangible form his selfish pride in his own power fades before a pure, unselfish pride in the thing he has created."

This view of the role of the fading ego in the creative process recalls to us Stephen Dedalus' Shelleyan pronouncement on the artist's mind as a fading coal in *Portrait*, just as the allegorical children bring to mind the contentious castle-making twins in the Nausicaa episode of *Ulysses*. Appearing first in *The Yale Review* in 1944, "The Sand Castle" has been criticized for its habit of subordinating story-telling to aesthetic polemics.[7] But making distinctions of an aesthetic and moral sort is natural to Lavin's art—*vide* the distinction between pleasure and happiness in "Happiness" or between death and pain in "The New Gardener." She is clearly a writer of intellectual speculation and moral force. For example, she puts forward a scathing picture of the clergy in "A Wet Day" while dramatizing the difference between rightness and righteousness—her main character is named Father Gogarty though he contrasts sharply to George Moore's sympathetic protagonist of that name in *The Lake*. The same perjorative view of the cloth pops up in "A Pure Accident" wherein the disintegrating priest, whose life has been "all boxes . . . confessional boxes, poor boxes, collection boxes, and pamphlet boxes," seems based on Joyce's Father Flynn who cracks up in the confessional box in "The Sisters." The use of clerical characters, of course, provides their creator with a good opportunity for moral conjecture and side-taking.

One final Lavin story, "The Widow's Son," is worth mentioning for its moral symbolism. Here Lavin tells first a straightforward tale of a lad's descent of a steep hill on his bicycle as he arrives home from school—alas, he swerves to avoid hitting a hen and is killed in the resulting accident before the horrified gaze of his adoring mother. How sad, the reader is signaled to feel; to lose so much in order to save so little. Lavin at this point intrudes upon the scene and says that she will tell the story over and this time save the lad Packy and kill the hen, for "After all, what I am about to tell you is no more of a fiction than what I have already told, and I lean no heavier now upon your credulity than, with your full consent, I did in the first instance." Besides, she explains, the art of both the story-teller and the gossip depend on the fact that it is easier to invent than to remember. In the retelling, though, Packy survives and tells his mother that he has won a scholarship. Thoughtlessly, she castigates him violently before the neighbors for killing her valuable hen, with the result that Packy runs away and never comes back.

The difference in the story's two versions, besides the apparent "changing" of the victim (the actual victim in both tellings is Packy), lies in the attitude of the mother who in the second version stupidly belittles her son rather than show publicly her pride in and love of him. In typical Lavin fashion, all the trouble comes from the mother's need to assert her modesty and stoicism and win the approval of the neighbors, "Them." "Perhaps," Lavin concludes, "all our actions have this double quality about them, this possibility of alternative, and it is only by careful watching and absolute sincerity, that we follow the path that is destined for us, and, no matter how tragic that may be, it is better than the tragedy we bring upon ourselves."

In this explicit disclosure of strong feeling, Lavin again shows the destructive propensities of communal opinion before which the mother in the story cowers. She also displays both her resignation toward the capriciousness of life and her vexation at the habit of human beings to themselves destroy their own lives. At the same time, she treats the reader to a disquisition on the privilege and dilemma of the artist in shaping a world and on her own need to ignore the imagined reaction of her audience. Down the hill of life races the man-child seeking to regain the womb, but such is possible only in death, the final box.

The retelling of the story allows Lavin to illustrate the powerful influence that tone and attitude have on plot and content: the change in the second version in the widow's attitude and the writer's tone toward the widow alters the reader's understanding of the story's meaning from simple regret to profound pity for those who meanly kill off love to win acceptance. What matters is the way the author wants to slant the mirror she holds up to life. The story, ultimately, like "The Sand Castle," is an *exemplum* of the primacy of art over life.

IV. "A Memory," the title story of the second last volume that Mary Lavin has published to date, seems to me a summative moment in her work. Thus, to recapitulate the habits just assigned to her, it is Joycean in overall form, using a James Duffy surrogate as anti-hero and developing along the lines of a sequel to "A Painful Case." It is Jamesian in the close attention it gives to social manners, psychological subtlety, stylistic richness, and dramatic use of point of view. It has moral force, humor, symbolism, sadness where there should be joy, self-deluded characters, and an awful woman.

In the story, the reclusive James, without last name, is prompted to leave his scholarly nook in rural Meath and come to Dublin by the sudden onset of sexual enthusiasm symbolized by the fire he carefully kindles and his general air of distraction and tenseness after "tossing around in the sheets till early morning." He is too peckish to work and heads for the sublimated hospitality of his city muse Myra, a sympathetic spirit who in James' opinion has the "verbal exactitude" of a man—her maleness is conveyed by her story of having sewn a gusset into her skirt in the lavatory of the National Library: "I'd turned it into trousers!" she claims proudly. Leaving his cottage, James passes the estate of his one-time girlfriend, Emmy (suggesting Emily Sinico), for whom, uniquely, he once entertained romantic desires that were almost violent in degree. Since then, like Mr. Duffy, and almost in Joyce's words, "marriage for him was out," being a low evasion of intellectual refinement; instead, "he came to believe that a man and a woman could enter into a marriage of minds."

For a time, it seems to the reader that mental Myra is the kind of model woman that Mr. Duffy wanted Mrs. Sinico to be, while the somatic Emmy is the kind that Mrs. Sinico was in actuality. But eventually Myra too reveals herself during her homeric argument with James to be only flesh and blood, a conventional aging woman with no longer repressible desires to be attended to by a man. James is exasperated "beyond belief" as Myra piteously flaunts her record of self-sacrifice in his service:

> 'So many, many years,' she whispered.
> It was only ten.[35]

James is totally flabbergasted that Myra would put their ethereal relationship on so common a basis as that of debt and gratitude. This broil over the teacups, which leaves James doddering and sputtering and the up-till-now adamantly circumspect Myra an hysterical wreck, is one of the most delicious scenes I know of in modern writing.

James is over-refined to the point of solipsism—refinement is his hideout against the degradation of fleshly imperatives. He never was able to bring himself to face a proper farewell scene with Emmy— instead, he sent her a curt note and left the country for two years. Now, altogether baffled by Myra's declaration that she has given him ten years of devotion for which she is awaiting reciprocation, James blunders out of her bungalow, empty of heart and stomach, and into the grounds of Emmy's estate when he loses his way home. His inability to follow the directions of the bus conductor is an indication of his failure to heed the world and of his lifelong habits of repression and self-delusion cultivated as if they were a higher calling. James that afternoon comes out of the darkness of the cinema to seek the platonic light of Myra whom he has "denatured," and he ends up in the darkness of the woods at Asigh House seeking the actual light of Emmy's window—but the darkness is to be his permanent condition, and he dies at the end with a mouth full of rotten leaves, all light, including the green one in the sky, having abandoned him.

James is a supreme self-fictionist, and Lavin makes him the dominant consciousness for all of the story except for the argument scene when the story is seen through Myra's eyes, enabling us to detect that she is not a personification of Holy Wisdom, as she has James thinking, but just a superannuated maiden wondering how soon she can relax and seek a few comforts like everybody else. Lavin's management of point of view here is one of her best achievements: both main characters win our sympathy and faith in their importance, yet both are unreliable in what they outwardly attest. In their hidden

hearts, they love one another, but, being "above" love, they can't admit
it. What could be sadder? How poignantly Lavin signals their true
feelings when Myra attempts to give James "a kiss of gratitude for
being you":

> Lightly she laid her cheek against his, while he for his part
> took her hand and stroked it. It was one of the more
> exquisite pleasures she gave him, the touch of her cool skin.
> His own hands had a tendency to ge thot although he
> constantly wiped them with his handkerchief. He had
> always preferred being too cold to being too hot.

Lavin uses windows and doors throughout the story to indicate James' sequestration. He sees the door of Myra's house shut
against him, and the gate of the National Library, and the bus entry-
way as the bus tries to pull away without him, and then Emmy's door
is dark. He is lost in the middle of the woods, like Dante, and repulsed
by nature, like Mr. Duffy being ejected from the edenic garden at the
end of "A Painful Case." Duffy sees the lovers in Phoenix Park lying
on the grass and knows that he can never emulate them; James sees the
leavings of the lovers in Emmy's wood. The window that he gallantly
opened when he first met Emmy is counterbalanced by repeated
closures as his life shuts down. He goes to his death astonished, like
Ivan Ilyich, that it could be happening to him. He dies with his
magnum opus unfinished, his mouth full of actual leaves while empty
of all the page leaves he has left unwritten, a mock fertility god. One
cannot help thinking of him as a Chekhovian comic character, a
learned child of inviolable innocence, a humbug who ignores the
vulgar world while craving its plaudits, as we see in his encounters
with the gate-keeper at the library and the bus conductor. He is the
comic stereotype of the absent-minded professor taken up by a writer
of genius and shown as if for the first time. James tells Myra at the
climax of their argument that " . . . there's nothing for me to do but
leave," and Lavin adds in counterpoint: "There seemed nothing left to
do but hit him."[37]

Mary Lavin is in the first rank of Irish short story writers for her
glorious power of always knowing the best thing to do next.

Notes

[1] V. S. Pritchett, Introduction to *Collected Stories* by Mary Lavin (Boston: Houghton-Mifflin, 1971), p. xii.

[2] Mary Lavin, *St. Stephen's [Magazine]*, (Trinity Term, No. 12, 1967), 22.

[3] Joyce, *Dubliners*, p. 112.

[4] Augustine Martin, "A Skeleton Key to the Stories of Mary Lavin," *Studies* (Winter, 1963), 398.

[5] Trains as symbols of mental and social compartmentalization appear, as we have seen, in O'Connor's "In the Train" and O'Faolain's "Up the Bare Stairs."

[6] Both A. A. Kelly (*Mary Lavin: Quiet Rebel* [New York: Barnes and Noble, 1980], p. 73) and Richard F. Peterson (*Mary Lavin* [Boston: Twayne Publishers, 1978], p. 26) deal with this emasculation symbol.

[7] See, *e.g.*, Zack Bowen's viewpoint in *Mary Lavin* (Lewisburg: Bucknell University Press, 1975), p. 55.

Bibliography

Moore, George. *The Untilled Field*. Toronto: Macmillan of Canada Limited, 1976.

Joyce, James. *Dubliners*. New York: Viking Press, 1961.

O'Connor, Frank. *Guests of the Nation*. London: Macmillan, 1931.

—. *Bones of Contention and Other Stories*. (London: Macmillan, 1936.

—. *Collection Two*. London: Macmillan, 1964.

—. *Collection Three*. London: Macmillan, 1969; published in U. S. as *A Set of Variations*. New York: Alfred A. Knopf, 1969.

—. *The Common Chord*. London: Macmillan, 1947.

—. *Crab Apple Jelly*. London: Macmillan, 1944.

—. *More Stories by Frank O'Connor*. New York: Alfred A. Knopf, 1954, 1967.

—. *Selected Stories*. Dublin: Maurice Fridberg, 1946.

—. *The Stories of Frank O'Connor*. New York: Alfred A. Knopf, 1952; London: Hamish Hamilton, 1953.

—. *Three Tales*. Dublin: Cuala Press, 1941.

—. *Traveller's Samples*. London: Macmillan, 1951.

O'Faolain, Sean. *The Collected Stories*. London: Constable, 1980; Boston: Atlantic, Little, Brown, 1983.

—. *The Finest Stories of Sean O'Faolain*. Boston: Little, Brown, 1957; republished as *The Stories of Sean O'Faolain*. London: Rupert Hart-Davis, 1958.

—. *Foreign Affairs and Other Stories*. London: Constable, 1976; Boston: Little, Brown, 1976.

—. *The Heat of the Sun: Stories and Tales*. London: Rupert Hart-Davis, 1966; Boston: Little, Brown, 1966.

—. *I Remember, I Remember!* Boston: Little, Brown, 1961; London: Rupert Hart-Davis, 1962.

—. *Midsummer Night Madness and Other Stories.* London: Jonathan Cape, 1932; New York: Viking Press, 1932.

—. *A Purse of Coppers: Short Stories.* London: Jonathan Cape, 1937; New York: Viking Press, 1938.

—. *Selected Stories of Sean O'Faolain.* London: Constable, 1978; Boston: Little, Brown, 1978.

—. *The Talking Trees and Other Stories.* Boston: Little, Brown, 1970; London: Jonathan Cape, 1971.

—. *Teresa and Other Stories.* London: Jonathan Cape, 1947; enlarged as *The Man Who Invented Sin and Other Stories.* New York: Devin-Adair, 1948.

O'Flaherty, Liam. *Duil (Desire).* Dublin: Sairseal agus Dill, 1953.

—. *The Fairy Goose and Two Other Stories.* New York: Gaige, 1927; London: Faber and Gwyer, 1927.

—. *The Mountain Tavern and Other Stories.* London: Jonathan Cape, 1929; New York: Harcourt, Brace, 1929.

—. *The Pedlar's Revenge.* Dublin: Wolfhound Press, 1975.

—. *Red Barbara and Other Stories.* New York: Gaige, 1928; London: Faber and Gwyer, 1928.

—. *The Short Stories of Liam O'Flaherty.* London: Jonathan Cape, 1937.

—. *Spring Sowing.* London: Jonathan Cape, 1924; New York: Alfred A. Knopf, 1926.

—. *The Stories of Liam O'Flaherty.* New York: Devin-Adair, 1956.

—. *The Tent.* London: Jonathan Cape, 1926.

—. *Two Lovely Beasts and Other Stories.* London: Victor Gollancz, 1948; New York: Devin-Adair, 1950.

—. *The Wild Swan and Other Stories.* London: Jackson, 1932.

—. *The Wounded Cormorant and Other Stories.* New York: W. W. Norton, The Norton Library, 1973.

Lavin, Mary. *At Sallygap and Other Stories.* Boston: Little, Brown, 1947.

—. *The Becker Wives and Other Stories*. London: Michael Joseph, 1946.

—. *Collected Stories*. Boston: Houghton Mifflin, 1971.

—. *The Great Wave and Other Stories*. London and New York: Macmillan, 1961.

—. *Happiness and Other Stories*. London: Constable, 1969; Boston: Houghton Mifflin, 1970.

—. *In the Middle of the Fields and Other Stories*. London: Constable, 1967; New York: Macmillan, 1969.

—. *The Long Ago and Other Stories*. London: Michael Joseph, 1944.

—. *Mary Lavin: Selected Stories*. Harmondsworth, U.K.: Penguin, 1981.

—. *A Memory and Other Stories*. London: Constable, 1972; Boston: Houghton Mifflin, 1973.

—. *The Patriot Son and Other Stories*. London: Michael Joseph, 1956.

—. *Selected Stories*. New York: Macmillan, 1959.

—. *The Shrine and Other Stories*. London: Constable, 1977; Boston: Houghton Mifflin, 1977.

—. *A Single Lady and Other Stories*. London: Michael Joseph, 1951.

—. *The Stories of Mary Lavin*, volume 1. London: Constable, 1964.

—. *The Stories of Mary Lavin*, volume 2. London: Constable, 1974.

Index

The following abbreviations after the names of the short stories indicate the volume in which each may be found:

Frank O'Connor:
CAJ	*Crab Apple Jelly*
GOTN	*Guests of the Nation*
TCC	*The Common Chord*
BOC	*Bones of Contention*
CS	*Collected Stories*
SBFO	*Stories by Frank O'Connor*
ASOV	*A Set of Variations*
CT	*Collection Two*

Sean O'Faolain:
CS	*Collected Stories*

Liam O'Flaherty:
SOLO	*The Stories of Liam O'Flaherty*
SSOLO	*The Short Stories of Liam O'Flaherty*
TLB	*Two Lovely Beasts*
TYR	*The Yale Review*, 1952

Mary Lavin:
H	*Happiness*
IMF	*In the Middle of the Fields*
SS	*Selected Stories*
TS	*The Shrine*
CS	*Collected Stories*
AM	*A Memory and Other Stories*
SML	*The Stories of Mary Lavin*